Encounters with the Irrational

Other Publications by the Same Author

Depression and creativity. International Universities Press, New York, 1985.

Parental loss and achievement. International Universities Press, Madison, CT, 1989. (with Eisenstadt, M., Rentchnick, P., de Senarclens, P.)

Fanaticism. A historical and psychoanalytical study. Schocken, New York, 1983. (with Molnar, M., Puymege, G. de)

Psychoanalysis and the sciences. Epistemology - History. Karnac, London and The University of California Press, Berkeley, 1993.

100 Years of Psychoanalysis. Contributions to the History of Psychoanalysis. Cahiers Psychiatriques Genevois, Special Issue, distribution Karnac, London, 1994. (with Falzeder, E.)

The technique at issue. Controversies in psychoanalysis from Freud and Ferenczi to Michael Balint. Karnac, London, 1988.

Controversies in psychoanalytic method. From Freud and Ferenczi to Michael Balint. New York University Press, New York, 1989.

Disappearing and Reviving. Sándor Ferenczi in the History of Psychoanalysis. London, Karnac, 2002.

(Under the supervision of), and "Introduction", in: *The Correspondence of Sigmund Freud and Sándor Ferenczi*, vol. 1-3. The Belknap Press/Harvard University Press, Cambridge, Mass., 1994-1996.

Encounters with the Irrational

My Story

André E. Haynal

with an interview by Judit Mészáros

Encounters with the Irrational: My Story
Copyright © 2017 by André E. Haynal
© Judit Mészáros, for her text in the interview.

International Psychoanalytic Books (IPBooks),
30-27 33rd Street, #3R
Astoria, NY 11102
Online at: www.IPBooks.net

All rights reserved. No part of this book may be used or reproduced in any manner whatsoever including Internet usage, without written permission of the author.
Translation of an interview and "A Psychoanalyst Listening to Fanatics":
Thomas A. Williams
Redactional assistance: Véronique D. Haynal
Redactional consultation: Sarah Wang

Parts of a recorded conversation with Ernst Falzeder, Ph.D. were taken over from a hitherto unpublished book project (2014) with permission of Dr. Ernst Falzeder to whom I express here my deep-felt thanks.

Cover design by Kathy Kovacic
Interior book design by Maureen Cutajar
Back cover by Lawrence L. Schwartz

ISBN: 978-0-9985323-1-8

Acknowledgements

I would like to express my sincere thanks to Judit Mészáros, Ph.D., psychoanalyst, member of the IPA, for the interview which is the backbone of this book. She played a major role in reintroducing me to the psychoanalytic, and broader cultural, life of Hungary and, in doing so, helped to alleviate some of the difficulties of my symbolic "homecoming," which allowed me to see again a country which I had fully lost in forty years of absence and to which I had difficulties in reconnecting

to Thomas A. Williams, Professor of English at the University of Szeged, for his excellent translation, which encompasses not only my admiration for his stylistic skills, including the right reproduction of the nuances of the original text, but also a grateful appreciation of his profound knowledge of the Central European cultural and historical environments, which helped me in developing the political, geographical, and historical landscape that is the backdrop to this text

to Sarah Wang, Ed.M., who accepted to take on her delicate shoulders all the chaos of these words, gathered into what I thought would be an *original text,* an *Ur-Text* after *Goethe's Urpflanzen,* a text from which others might take their form, but has since become, thanks to her, a shining piece of precious metal—to my own surprise. Her sensitivity and her knowledge were essential for allowing the text to transform into what it is. I am very thankful to her

to Ernst Falzeder Ph.D., such an ancient relationship, especially important at the time and in the preparation of the publication of the

Freud-Ferenczi Correspondence. He has become so close a friend that the excerpts from our conversations added to this text are just a drop in the sea of what I have received from him as stimulation, invigoration, and inspiration between friends who have indeed become like brothers

for the tireless dactylographic preparation of different versions and modifications of this text and for the composition of the bibliography, my gratefulness goes to Sophie Cazillac

for feedbacks and critical remarks, all my thanks go to Gabriela Schäppi and Jean-Michel Quinodoz (Geneva) as well as Christina Griffin and Judith Vida (Los Angeles, California), Axel Hoffer (Brookline, MA), Cleo Haynal (Virginia Beach, VA) as well as Antoine and Danielle Maurice (Geneva)

to Véronique D. Haynal, M.A., with whom, after thirty-two years of intensive sharing of life, emotions and thinking, we end up not knowing exactly which ideas, impressions, and thoughts belong to one or the other. Thus she is, in fact, a co-author of this book. Moreover, she inspired and encouraged ideas and powerfully helped to find the words for their expression. This work became in *many* senses a *labor of love*

Special acknowledgment: a different and complete version of the interview with Judit Mészáros appeared in Haynal, A., Mészáros, J.: *Nemek és igenek*. Budapest, Oriold, 2012.

Table of Contents

PROLOGUE... 1
   First Scene. The Cast.................................. 1
   My Primary Interest: the Irrational.................... 2
   Sincerity.. 3
   Concentric Circles..................................... 3

1. THE IRRATIONAL SPRINGING FORTH 7
   How to Write about Oneself?............................ 7
   Transylvanian Roots 8
   Strong Heads.. 11
   Landing in Budapest, (1919-39)........................ 17
   Mother, or the Fate of the Very Last One 20
   Transylvania Calls my Father 29
   A Mysterious "Illness"................................ 30
   War and Occupation (1944-45).......................... 36
   After the War—The Leaden Years........................ 43
   Student Life: Learning and Socializing 48
   There is No Great Future Here for Me.................. 50
   Terra Firma after Directionless Navigation............ 55
   Onward: Preparation................................... 56
   Zurich.. 59
   Euphoria was Gradually Replaced by the Doldrums....... 61

2. DEPRESSION AND CREATIVITY 69
   The Meaning of Despair 69

3. THE GUIDANCE OF THE IRRATIONAL 77
   "Transfer" (Über-tragung). 77
   Psychoanalysis in Zurich 79
   Seeking a New Lifestyle. Discovering Geneva… 83
   Learning, and Re-Learning 93
   Psychoanalysis and the University. 102
   Technique and Method: The Psychoanalytical Practice. 105
   A Sojourn in North America, at Last. 111
   Back in Geneva, a New Life 116
   Slowly but Surely, the Family became Cosmopolitan: Kids 117
   Discovering a Serene Psychoanalyst: Ferenczi in Correspondence with Freud 124
   Supervisions in the European World 130
   Encounters with Colleagues in the World 131

4. A PSYCHOANALYST LISTENING TO FANATICS. 135
   Civilizations and their Illusions. 139
   What Accounts for the Appeal of Fanaticism?. 141
   Objections 142
   The Structure of Fanaticism, from its Birth on 143
   Simplified World 144
   Everyday Fanaticism 146
   Members of a Cult 147
   The Fanatics and their Group 150
   Outlook on our Epoch. 154
   The Initiator and the Follower. 157
   Seeds of Fanaticism in Psychoanalysis. 160
   Fanaticism Still Alive 164

EPILOGUE. 165

BIBLIOGRAPHICAL REFERENCES 169

List of Illustrations

Figure 1: Family Gejza Haynal.................................. 9
Figure 2: Aunt Róza.. 12
Figure 3: 1921 Versailles Treaty............................... 14
Figure 4: Prof. Imre Haynal, my father........................ 16
Figure 5: Professor Sándor Koranyi............................ 18
Figure 6: Margit Haynal, my mother............................ 20
Figure 7: Dear Fräulein Milli and little André................ 24
Figure 8: Father and son (Imre and André)..................... 27
Figure 9: Dr. Imre Haynal at Hospital Rókus with his team..... 28
Figure 10: Newly built house in Buda, 1940.................... 32
Figure 11: André with puli dogs Bolhás and Füstös............. 33
Figure 12: St Imre high school in Buda........................ 35
Figure 13: My class in St Imre high school.................... 37
Figure 14: André's only diary during the siege of Budapest.... 40
Figure 15: Budapest in 1945: Bridge over the Danube........... 41
Figure 16: Budapest in 1945................................... 42
Figure 17: 1956: André in an anti-Soviet demonstration........ 49
Figure 18: André and the University Neurological Clinic, Zurich...... 63
Figure 19: Prof. Julian de Ajuriaguerra in Geneva............. 85
Figure 20: Professor Julian de Ajuriaguerra dancing........... 86
Figure 21: Raymond de Saussure................................ 94
Figure 22: Marcelle Spira..................................... 94
Figure 23: Marcelle Spira and Paul Parin discussing........... 95
Figure 24: Michael Balint.................................... 112
Figure 25: Daughter Cleo born June 1985...................... 118
Figure 26: Son David born March 1987......................... 119
Figure 27: Anne-Marie and Joe Sandler listening to Paul Parin....... 132
Figure 28: «Fanaticism» book review on *Le Monde*............ 137
Figure 29: Sigmund Freud's Conference about Fanaticism....... 150

Prologue

First Scene. The Cast

An autumn day: a bright and beautiful September Saturday in Budapest.

André: Yes, it is a wonderful stage.

Judit: Stage?

André: In fact…. Here we are, sitting on Szent István Boulevard under the weeping fig tree, at your home.

Judit: We're attempting to fulfill an old idea of ours—the game. We just talk, and lighter topics lead to a more profound exchange of ideas. So we thought, "Why not record these conversations?"

It's like keeping a journal. You begin with writing things down for yourself, and it suddenly occurs to you that you may be writing for the future, for others.

André: For the future or the present?

Judit: Perhaps it doesn't really matter. At some point, you realize you're writing for others. From now on, we'll carry on our conversation knowing that we may be sharing it with others.

André: One always writes for an audience.

There were several meetings over the years between us; and the complete interview was published in another format in the original Hungarian (Haynal, Mészáros, 2012).

Judit is a well-known psychoanalyst and professor at the University Eötvös in Budapest, Hungary, who has spent the duration of her life in this city, even during some dreadful political events. As for me, I chose another life's path, emigration. In recalling, 55 years later, my memories from this definitive time period, I came to realize that I had followed a pattern, willingly or not, that nearly all of my forefathers had also followed. Practically none of them died in the place where he was born. This may not have been a conscious motivation on my part; I only just discovered it in reflecting on my own life. This "discovery" has lead me to demonstrate that life is not a linear path, well-lit by conscious, thought-out decisions, but is marked by turns, creative twists, surprises much stranger than fiction. Some of these unforeseeable, sometimes even surprising for the one who lives them, movements come from the interior world and follow a plan, an unconscious map, suggested in dreams, the irresponsible whims and fancies, the wanderings of the mind... There is also always chance, but that is another topic.

My Primary Interest: the Irrational

Here I am, explicitly speaking about myself and my encounters with the irrational influences in my life. I realized that researching the irrationality hidden in my fate is one of the leitmotifs of my life. What I call "irrational" are those thoughts and attitudes that do not follow the logic of the foreseeable, expectable sequence, and their resulting events. We all *fear* the irrational—therefore it was always put outside of the science (e.g. dreams). Hence, the aversion accompanying Freud's scrutiny of one part of the irrational—the unconscious, which has a tendency to take shape without being explicitly pre-thought. Furthermore, the irrational also encompasses other mysterious phenomena e.g. coincidental, unexpected meetings (as mine with Etelka in Vienna, which was decisive for my settling in Switzerland for nearly my whole life), or phenomena called "parapsychological" (see Lloyd Mayer, 2007)[1] which includes telepathy and also what some psychoanalysts consider a part of "transference" i.e. a non-conscious and non-controlled aspect in the relation. The pioneers, Freud, Jung and Ferenczi were fascinated by these kinds of events as recorded in their lively correspondence. Others (E. Jones) considered these marginal occurrences as unworthy of including in scientific exploration although they appear even in situations of clinical communication.

SINCERITY

The intimacy between two psychoanalysts who occasionally discuss their work and their personal reactions to it creates, in principle, an atmosphere of sincerity. I mean "in principle" because difficulties emerge while putting it into practice: what will my wife say in reading this? Do I want my children to know everything? Or my colleagues? Or my patients? It is true that, little by little, I am putting more of myself into this writing.

People sometimes think that the analysts speak about the others, their client, their "patients" or, at worst, their "case". "It is high time that the analysts begin to speak about themselves" is a remark I have often heard. In fact, I observed that we, analysts, are mainly speaking about ourselves, our perception of our encounter with others.

CONCENTRIC CIRCLES

Even if I overcome the obstacles to a quasi-total transparency, ultimately, what is the purpose of recording what I think? I hope that the reader may find it within the initial circle of my conversation with Judit, in the sections that I have chosen to include, and which are in italics to differentiate them from the rest of the text. Moreover, I added some reminiscences of conversations with my colleague and friend Ernst

---

[1] A fascinating presentation of a broad series of scientific research about these phenomena under the very evocative title "*Extraordinary Knowing*" by Elisabeth Lloyd Mayer.

Falzeder (text marked in italics), to whom I also narrated some old stories, which could help illustrate the rest of the text. These are what Freud called *Einfälle*, rather simplistically translated as "free associations" ["incursion" would be a better rendering of the connotation of the term]. As a matter of fact, I feel free to take my own approach presenting my life in concentric circles. The conversations with Judit and Ernst, the *Einfälle*, are encompassed by a second circle: a *commentary*, where my life's narrative is more clearly organized. From there, a *communication* as the continuation of a meditation; here, a new character, the reader, also takes his place, as his presence and his silent attention is also discernible.

In the next and third circle, we take under closer examination, two chosen focal themes which have made themselves known again and again throughout life: *depression and creativity* and their relationship to each other, and *fanaticism*. And I would venture to say that these two issues do not only present themselves in my own life, but are there as well for many of the rest of us, and even pervade our society on the whole.

Depression is deeply embedded in the solitude of my childhood, followed by unexpected changes in my family, separations and war, persecution and exile. On a fine day in Zurich, a question arose from within me: "If I disappeared altogether, would anyone notice?" This little book may be part of the response in the *depression-creativity* spectrum. This writing belatedly shows that I existed there, at the time, seated on my couch, and today it is my creativity that substantiates this existence. Moreover, I will take a moment to speak about depression in everyday life—the general discontent, which saturates life in our society, in people who try to put up with unavoidable changes that rarely fulfill their promises. I have found that depression inspires creativity in my own life, in order to fight dangerous depressive inactivity. Therefore, the books that I have created have kept me company.

Fanaticism also finds its own deep roots in my early life: the anti-fanatic attitudes of my parents, of my teachers at school and of my later environment, provide stark contrast to the spectacle of incredible horrors inflicted by fanatics in the country of my birth. Nowadays, I notice it not only in foremost political and ideological convictions, but it has become more and more striking to me that in our so-called "civilized" society, fanatical mentality subtly infiltrates daily life and personal convictions—some of which seem so commonplace or shared by so many—in tiny doses of poison injected into daily exchanges. It bears witness to the omnipresence of *envy* and *jealousy* and draws us back to the complex problem of competition and drive to power. Nowadays we can scarcely have a conversation with somebody without feeling the ghost of political correctness. But when we maintain that a sentence is politically correct, to which political doctrine are we adhering? In general, clarification is avoided. Various remnants or real convictions of nationalism, chauvinism, xenophobia, racism or religious extremism are hidden beneath innocent quips and tentative opinions. I attempted to clarify the mechanisms at play here in using my understanding of clinical encounters with fanatic people to extrapolate and illuminate similar everyday attitudes and ways of thinking.

In my opinion, psychology and psychoanalysis can make our life more transparent, understandable, and less dominated or overwhelmed by the underlying emotions of fear, hatred, envy, aggression, and the desire for dominance, thus opening the door to a more harmonious, more satisfying life.

All of this reminds me of my son, who, at the age of eight or nine, surprised me with a thought, saying: "Papa, you have had a troubled life, you should write about it."

Now, twenty years later, I am following his advice, and I wonder: Was it just "trouble" or was it not also instructive, exciting, stimulating, provoking my curiosity and posing intriguing questions about open problems? All in all, my life was fascinating. I learned that life is rational, but mind is irrational, and I comprehended how the irrational manifests itself in life—there is a great deal of irrationality in my own life. There is a great deal of it in the world, in each of us; there is also chance which is the irrational in meeting between our behavior and our mind as well as in the craziness of our world. I endeavored to tease out an understanding of these interactions in myself and out of hundreds of patients over the years, letting me understand how these irrationalities coexists and interact and influence one another. Thinking about my existence accompanied me in fact as an object of eagerness. I hoped that, in understanding myself, I might better understand others, in our all similarities and differences, as they are each, in fact, my sister or brother.

The references, the exciting discoveries of modern psychology revealing more and more of the hidden aspects of our inner lives give me a kind of epistemological basis. I became enthusiastic about the exploration of our *mind* from the early discoveries in the field: the new vision proposed by Freud followed by the recent discoveries in connection with the underlying neurological hardware, the sciences of the *brain*. The arc encompassing my associations of thoughts from the start to now lead me to reflect and meditate about two fundamental problems, essential enigmas of contemporary human existence in our culture, depression and fanaticism, and they became important points of my narrative. In thinking about myself, I succeeded to sum up what I have learned about the other people with whom I shared my existence.

Finally, with time, the psychological barriers that would have previously hindered me from speaking about myself so forthrightly have begun to fade away.

I hope that the reader will share my pleasure in turning up, down, and around the things and thoughts that are still searching for their place in my mind as much as in our modern world.

1

... the Irrational Springing Forth

How to Write about Oneself?

How may we present ourselves to others? How well do we even know ourselves? Or, are we discovering parts of ourselves at various moments of our own history? In psychoanalysis, we presume that we do not actually know our own personality entirely—as Freud's works implies; we can recognize various layers—this is what postmodern psychoanalysts believe, such as W.R. Bion and others, and myself included.[2] Nevertheless, we still know in a particular moment how to think about ourselves—my personal reality at this instant. After the self-reflective works of Augustine, Montaigne, Proust, and others, there seems to be little more interesting than to think about ourselves, as eventually we come to understand others through ourselves. I can hope that these lines will interest others, thanks to their own identification and dis-identification. Leaving further generalizations behind, let us follow the remark of Paul Valéry, reminding us that, if we want to swim in the sea, we must first jump into the water.... Here I jump into the stream of my reminiscences.

---

[2] In other words, Freud thought that there is a "second person" hiding behind each person. Today, it is believed that there are *many others* hiding behind that person.

The early childhood environment largely determines our lives—according to the idea asserted by many from Freud to Erik Erikson and Daniel N. Stern and even contemporary neurobiologists like Eric Kandel. This was as true as it could be for someone born the only child into a family of physicians in the 1930s in Central Europe, especially if the parents kept their eye on, discouraged, even frowned upon his every step, lest that step take him away from the family. They even strictly forbade him from taking such steps. The question naturally arises as to whether all of this had anything to do with the parents' and relatives' own search for identity, and the social, and other (professional and political), uncertainties surrounding them; there was a great deal of uncertainty indeed. I was educated under a cloud of anxiety. But it is also conceivable that we see it this way only in hindsight today after having developed sensitivities to such wavelengths.

Here, things have already become intricate. To keep things simple, let's begin with a sociological and historical picture of my father's family.

Transylvanian Roots

My family has Transylvanian roots. The first figure that I know of is my great-great-great-great-grandfather from the 1600s. He was made a member of the gentry for his military service under prince Gábor Bethlen. This ancestor fought the Ottomans in the Carpathian Mountains—he wasn't the only one in the family to do so—and received a title for meritorious service in battle. It was a military nobility, not one that came with land and feudalism. Since, as a result, the family was fortunately not granted an estate, many of them became judges and doctors in the nineteenth century. That is, they belonged to the small, primarily Transylvanian social stratum whose members lived as intellectual, mobile professionals as early as the nineteenth century. My grandfather, Gejza (old form of Géza) Haynal, was a doctor, the head of a hospital in Beszterce, and a pediatrician. When Béla Bartók was still a child living in Transylvania,[3] my grandfather was his

---

[3] Béla Bartók (1881–1941), the Hungarian composer and pianist who is considered among the most important composers of the twentieth century, was born in the small

doctor (Szegő, 1965). By that time the child had learned how to play the piano from his father. When little Béla's father died, my grandfather would ask him to play for him each time he came over to see him. It's as if my grandfather had been a "psychotherapist" before the word was coined, and was concerned with his musical evolution. Beszterce was then a Saxon Lutheran town, where German was the language of public administration, and, as an independent, free royal town, could practically do whatever it wanted in political and administrative independence.

Figure 1: Family Gejza Haynal

From this time on, the history of my family played out in two places: the early beginnings take place in Transylvania (which was then a part of Hungary), until around 1848, and were followed by different moves of parts of the family, first to Valachia (which would become a part of Romania), and eventually to Hungary in the twentieth century.

The leading socio-cultural layer in Transylvania was Hungarian, a Calvinist (Reformed Church) majority that lived in harmony with Hungarian Catholics, the Orthodox Romanians, the Lutheran Germans (in *pars pro toto*, all ethnic Germans in Transylvania were called Saxons, in contrast to the "Danubian Swabians," which were those ethnic Germans who lived in Habsburg-controlled Hungary); furthermore there were Armenians and Jews, who

---

town of Nagyszentmiklós, in Transylvania, known as Sânnicolau Mare in present-day Romania.

both followed their own ancient religions. This area was long an island of tolerance, even during the Thirty Years' War—a time during which the birth of a constitution more or less cemented this status quo. It was around this period that a real little Switzerland could have been created in the middle of the Carpathian Mountains, if this process had not been halted[4] early on by the Habsburgs' reoccupying territories and supporting the Counter-Reformation. In the middle of the 19th Century, a strong nationalistic influence spread from Hungary, disturbing the previously peaceful atmosphere. As a result, the Transylvanian Hungarians often rather opted for emigration. Indeed, my family left Transylvania in the second part of the 19th Century to a territory eastward, beyond the Carpathian Mountains, which did not belong to the Habsburg Kingdom of Hungary, called the Vlach Regat, that is "Old Romania."[5] They settled in the much less developed Bukovina. Later, after some important changes in the existing political order, the family came back to Transylvania (in Hungary) at the end of the 19th Century.

It is interesting to see that communities tend to maintain their own social circles elsewhere in the world. This is no different today. Every major city around the globe consists of numerous microcosms, and among them the Transylvanian as well. For foreigners, Hungarians are simply Hungarians; but this is a one-sided view. In Switzerland people are identified as, for example, Niederwaldians, Lucernians, or Genevians; in Germany as, for example, Bavarians, Prussians, or Rhinelanders; similarly, on closer inspection the sociological, traditional, and other differences between people from outside of Budapest, people from Budapest, and people within different sections of Budapest are as significant, if not more so than, those between people from Vienna, Berlin, Zurich, and Frankfurt.

It is important to note this because I became conscious only later of the fact that I had actually grown up in a micro-society that can be well delineated. Since my father worked as the only goy (gentile) in a clinic

---

[4] If "if" has any meaning in history it refers to a dream of desire and not historical reality (or historical possibility).

[5] Regatul Vechi, or Regat, was the name for the area beyond the Carpathians in Romania that formed part of Romania even before World War I, after which Romanian territory was expanded significantly.

for internal medicine (Baron Sándor Korányi's clinic), for my whole childhood, I was surrounded almost exclusively by the children of his Jewish colleagues. In the world in which I lived, I never heard about origin, race, or religious differences until they became tragically important when the Germans occupied the country in 1944.

STRONG HEADS

For the time being, however, let us stay with my immediate family and the stories and myths that they maintained. The less mythical facts reach back to the nineteenth century. Independent-mindedness was displayed already in the family. For example during an anti-Jewish pogrom, the Haynals were living on a farm in Botoșani, Bukovina at the time. My grandparents got out their hunting rifle to protect the people who lived near to them—these Jews—since there was no significant government authority there. I think they sort of did what they felt they had to do.

My Aunt Róza participated in the anti-Habsburg conspiracy organized by Blanka Teleki, for which, in 1849, after Hungary's War of Independence was crushed, she was locked up in the Kufstein Prison in Tyrol. The Austrians obviously had no idea what to do with female prisoners and released Aunt Róza, but only after three years. She was one of the earliest female politicians: today she might even be said to have been a feminist. From then on, in the family, anti-Habsburg sentiments ran deep. They said my great-grandfather, for example, had hung a picture of Kaiser Franz Joseph in the toilet and told some gendarmes searching his home: "I like him so much that I even need to look at him here."

One of my uncles joined the Ottoman army because of his antipathy for the Russians in order to fight on what he considered the "right" side later as an officer in the Crimean War. The rebellious character that occasionally broke with tradition and was incapable of submission has obviously been reproduced again and again in the family. Would this perhaps be the "irrational transgenerational crypt" of which a few Ferenczi[6] followers, such

---

[6] Sándor Ferenczi (1873-1933): in my eyes the closest follower and quasi friend of Freud's, whose important work was a major object of my scientific scrutiny (see last chapter of this text).

Figure 2: Aunt Róza

as Nicolas Abraham (Paris), spoke about? Nor did this character trait fade in my father—neither during the time of the German occupation in 1944, nor in the Stalinist years that followed soon after, as the behavior of my father during those times bears witness.

Earlier, my father had completed his university studies in 1916 in Kolozsvár and was drafted to the Hungarian Army. It was during that time that he met Charles[7], the future king of Hungarians, when Charles visited his regiment [and he wrote about it later in his war journal]. The doctors, who were also officers, were introduced to him. This particular regiment was mainly composed of German speakers. Charles then asked to my father, "Haynal, das ist doch ein ungarischer Name, nicht wahr?" To which my father answered, "Ja, ich bin ein Ungar."[8] That is the story of his audience with the future king, Charles. Much later when my father came to Geneva we went to the lakeshore—where Elisabeth, the highly popular Austrian empress and Hungarian queen they called Sisi, had been killed—I was surprised to hearing him say, "This is where they killed our queen." For him Elisabeth was still "our queen" in 1973.

However, the Hapsburgs weren't always happy with him as, in the army, he realized that—based on a regulation of the time—those whose health had suffered to a certain degree had to be discharged. My father's courageous and nonconformist ways of thinking ran afoul of the military authorities when he applied their regulations by the letter and wanted to send home half the men under his charge, due to their poor health, but he was reported and court-martialed as a saboteur. I think he did it partially because of his pacifism, but it was also an obvious form of resistance against authority and for favoring independence of thought. During his court martial, he was acquitted since his only intention had been to follow regulations—that's what he rightfully argued. Since they couldn't leave it at that, he was transferred to a place where he wouldn't have the same authority. He ended up on the Serbian front and later got

---

[7] Charles I, the last Habsburg monarch, became the emperor of Austro-Hungary and the king of Hungary (1916-1918).
[8] "Haynal, that's a Hungarian name, isn't it?" "Yes, I'm Hungarian."

as far as the Isonzo,⁹ but, meanwhile, for some reason, he was also sent to Poland. I don't know the details. I only read it in his journal.

Just after WWI, my grandparents moved from Beszterce (Transylvania) to Budapest. So far, so good. It was impossible to find a place to live in Budapest at the time, so for a while they lived in a railroad car at one of the train stations.

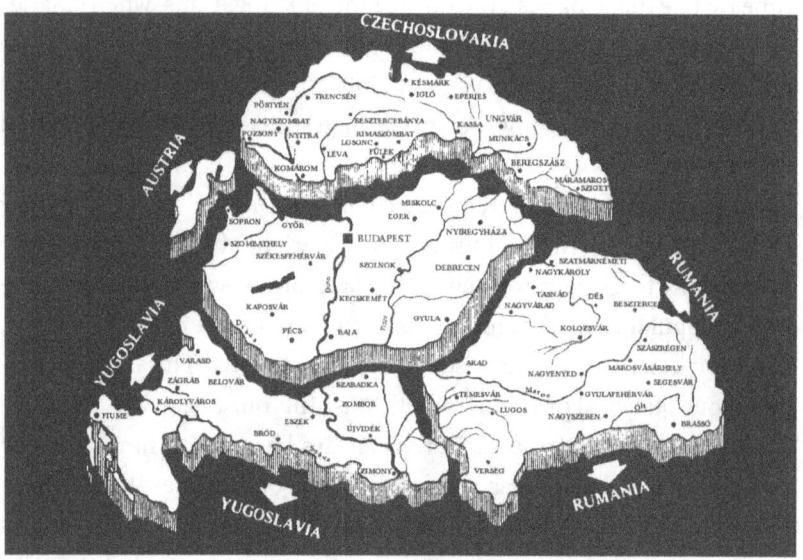

Figure 3: 1921 Versailles Treaty

Judit: *Did your father get into any other trouble?*

André: *He got into a great deal of trouble.*

Judit: *In the 1950s, too, in the Sántha affair...*¹⁰

André: *Right, right. That's why I said that the family history is interesting because he was headstrong and intractable – yes, I think*

---

⁹ A particularly terrible battlefront in the south.

¹⁰ Professor Sántha, an excellent Canada trained anti-Nazi neurosurgeon, was accused of belittling the Stakhanovism movement (imposing a maximum effort on the workers). He was expulsed from the University Clinic and exiled in a little province town where neurosurgical interventions could not be performed. My father was the only one who dared to stand up for him and protested against this false accusation and the subsequent mock trial and condemnation.

that's the word I was looking for. He was an intractable man.

Judit: Why don't we say that he stuck to his own principles?

André: With little inclination to compromise.

Judit: He took his own moral norms seriously, and those norms endured under any circumstances.

To Judit: André: That's right. In Hungary – well, I don't need to tell you – those norms have constantly been changing. My father was an excellent doctor and public person. He was admired by many for his courage, you could say that he behaved like a Pater Familias for his students, clinical collaborators and patients, he gave them the maximum protection he was able to provide. He was a highly intelligent and cultured man. He collected books of rare value and high interest; he ended up having the most unbelievable library in town. At home he imposed his will authoritatively; he devoted little time to all else that surrounded him, having only exceptional moments for his son. He was a strange man. To be frank, he was very strange. You'll see later. I'd say he traumatized others.

My daughter Cleo– whom I adore –and I, we checked some of the documents that were left to us, including those tied to my father and the family. We could see what life was like in my grandfather's time: one of his brothers graduated from high school in Chernovitsi, and his diploma says that he studied in German but that he also took his Matura exams in Polish and Romanian. That is, we were a typical Austro-Hungarian family. My grandmother was supposedly Polish, from the part of Poland that belonged to Austria at the time, Krakow, so I think that my father's resentment towards nationalism also reflected his emotions over the loss of a world. He'd say, "Under Horthy, we've become Balkan." Being "Balkan" signified a big demotion from "western Europe," represented then by the Habsburg Empire. That was something he'd regularly declare. The other statement he'd make was: "Hungarian nationalists prefer to belong to the Balkans than to Austria."

My grandmother spoke German with her children, and the children spoke Hungarian with their father—and Romanian with domestic and hospital staff. About this period, my family held memories of a happy world, which disappeared forever during the time of the three men—Horthy, Hitler, and Stalin—who, in the decades to come, would determine Hungary's fate.

Figure 4: Prof. Imre Haynal, my father

My father remained faithful to the German-speaking Lutheran community of the little Transylvanian town of Beszterce (Bistrița in present-day Romania) and, deep in his soul, was profoundly saddened over the collapse of the Austro-Hungarian Empire[11] and the provincialization of the country that followed, for which he blamed the stupid soldiers around Horthy—this is also supported by the memoirs of Horthy, whose simple-mindedness, in my opinion, was only superseded by his political stupidity. He and his supporters established a semi-fascist regime similar to most peripheral states in the Europe of that day (much like what Mussolini, Franco, Salazar, Piłsudski, and Mannerheim did in Italy, Spain, Portugal, Poland and Finland, respectively). My father could not stand this military-clerical

---

[11] Enlightened by the poignant accounts by Stefan Zweig and Joseph Roth.

regime and had a great deal of trouble with the authorities. When he was working at the Rókus hospital in Budapest,—as one of the chief physicians in internal medicine, in one of the oldest hospitals in Budapest, Rókus—he decided, based on an old regulation, to provide treatment free of charge for those who had little or no income at all. Consequently, he brought on himself endless complications in the 1930s. His Anglophile attitude also stood in sharp contrast to the Hungarian political system. Back in Hungary, my father then wrote the first book on cardiology in Hungarian, in 1938: Diseases of the Heart and Blood Vessels, for which he had to create the proper Hungarian terminology. If my mother had not spoken perfect Hungarian, my father, with his own German culture, would have had difficulty with this task. During that time, he kept running in and out of my mother's room, asking how you'd say this and how you'd spell that…. It wasn't easy.

LANDING IN BUDAPEST (1919-39)

It seems to me that an unjust law is no law at all.
AUGUSTINE

But let's go back to my father's arrival in Budapest just after the First World War. He went to the Korányi Clinic. At first, he made his living only by giving shots to members of rich families. He was running around the city, and he'd collect the little tips that he received that way. Then he moved to England with my mother thanks to the Rockefeller Grant. For a few years, they lived in London and he worked at Sir Thomas Lewis's clinic—he was among the first to study the possible diagnostic uses of the electrocardiogram (ECG). St. Thomas's Hospital was the first major cardiology clinic in England. The ECG was an innovation at the time, and a new functional cardiology started to develop, the first Hungarian witness to which was my father. As a result, as said, he later wrote the first Hungarian textbook in cardiology. Here is another encounter with the irrational. Imagine what it would have been if I was born during their stay in the UK: I would be a British subject and would have been spared of war in Central Europe and especially the occupations. My whole life would have been different. The real story is that my mother wanted to give birth in the presence of her mother and therefore my parents left Great Britain and returned to Budapest.

There he became the head of the Department of Internal Medicine at Rókus Hospital. Rókus was then considered one of the capital's great old hospitals, so he had a highly prestigious position particularly as a specialist in cardiology. When he became the chief physician at the Rókus Hospital, the Horthy regime closed the Korányi Clinic—one of the only institutes of major international standing in the country. Incidentally, it was that same Sándor Korányi who wrote the chapter on nephrology in the great and prestigious *Handbuch der inneren Medizin* (Textbook on Internal Medicine). When the clinic was closed, my father couldn't think of anything better to do than to take on his excellently trained former colleagues at Rókus.

Judit: He hired them and saved them in the process.

André: Yes, in the early thirties. Not in '44 or '38, but already in the early thirties. I still have the letter in which the state secretary wrote him that the matter was being viewed as a temporary measure and that people "of Jewish descent" could not remain at a public hospital.

Figure 5: Professor Sándor Koranyi

What happened then was that Sándor Korányi passed away on April 12, 1944, that is, a mere few weeks after the German occupation of the country began on March 19. Nobody wanted to say anything about him, so a couple of people were asked to write an obituary in the Orvosi Hetilap,[12] as was the practice at the time. Sándor Korányi had been the great figure and doyen of what was called Hungarian or Budapest internal medicine. It was impossible not to write about him, so they ended up asking my father. And, at the end of his article, he stated courageously that "if there was to be a Hungarian medical science, it would always be associated with the name of Korányi." The article was published.

To Ernst: Recently, someone quoted my father who said that there are situations in which the usual prohibitions do not apply, although I think in saying so he took up a thought of Churchill's. In any case, during the German occupation my father told the medical students that they could fill out as many fabricated certificates as they wished; they would only do something good. He could have been arrested for that. Today I am convinced that there was also much depression involved in this great courage of his. Presumably a life crisis, which he underwent at that time, contributed to this, as my parents no longer lived together ... Was there also a latent self-destructive tendency at play, which, however, enabled the rescue of many people? Would he have dared to do this had he been "reasonable"?

His behavior can be explained neither by his Catholic-liberal convictions, nor by his Anglophilia, nor by the fact that he had close Jewish friends. He had no personal motives to help particular people, perhaps with the exception of his brother-in-law, the husband of his sister, whom he liked very much. On various occasions he was not cautious enough, and that's when he "slipped". He should rather have acted in secrecy, which he was quite capable of in other situations.

---

[12] *Orvosi Hetilap* (Medical Weekly) is Hungary's most important and most widely circulated medical journal.

Mother, or the Fate of the Very Last One

Figure 6: Margit Haynal, my mother

André: My mother had fourteen siblings, including half-siblings.

Judit: Where did your mother fit in the birth order?

André: She was the second to the last. The last girl. My grandfather on my mother's side was the főispan, the chief of Szatmár County. That area was called Partium[13] and belonged to Transylvania, politically, though it was geographically part of the Hungarian Alföld region (called also the Puszta). Indeed, although both families were Transylvanian, sociologically they were very different. Members of my mother's family were "stiff-necked Calvinists," very keen on upholding tradition. Nevertheless, surprisingly, my grandfather on my mother's side got a divorce after having had some 11 children. I'm uncertain again, but, of course, there may be an unconscious reason why I usually get this wrong. Before the turn of the century, my grandfather lost everything when he got divorced. He left everything

---

[13] Named so because in an old Latin text of a peace treaty you can read: "Transylvaniae et partium ei annexarum" i.e. Transylvania and the parts which are added to it.

to his wife: farms of various sizes, which were not estates but still lands of significant size outside of Szatmár County, where he lived. I learned all this from my cousin when I was thirty. There were always uncles and aunts and cousins around, but I never understood the whole story until recently. Is that part of why I became a psychoanalyst? ... We were a "Freudian type of family" in a certain sense, a family in which the old men were referred to as my cousins and the young men as my uncles – or was it the other way around? I never really understood any of it.

My mother was the second-to-the-last child from the second marriage, and they got so fed up with her that they sent her away from Szatmár County, from her Calvinist family, to Veszprém, to the Catholic nuns, so they would bring her up. She often told us that she had to get up at six, they'd ring the bell, she'd stand in line to go to church, and then she'd be told that, as she was a heretic, she might as well stay behind. And that's what would repeat itself every morning.... Later, she attended a teacher's college, the old one set up in Pozsony (Pressburg, later Bratislava) in the days of the Austro-Hungarian Empire.

Judit: What is it that your mother succeeded in doing that they would have gotten so fed up with her?

André: It was that she was the nth child. My grandfather may really have had enough. And as for why I didn't like my grandmother, there was also a very simple reason: each summer they'd dump me down there, and there were 10 to 15 cousins – that's where the number 16 comes from. There were often 16 of us sitting around the table. My grandfather would sit down to have lunch exactly at 12, and the meal was served immediately. No one was ever late, and we were all there. And we were not allowed to talk. Only if Grandpa asked, "Andris, how are you?" then I'd say, "I am well, thank you." I was the youngest of the cousins. The others went riding and swimming in the Szamos. But the Szamos was considered too dangerous for me, and riding was anyhow out of the question because I might have fallen off the horse.

So I suffered the same fate as my mother did in that family – the fate of the very last one. Especially since I was from Budapest, which they really didn't like since, for them, Budapest was an alien city with different habits and linguistic expressions…

Judit: …sin city, as Horthy said. You spent the summers with your grandparents, and this lasted a couple of weeks.

André: The summer lasted two months. I spent one month at my grandmother's because I was left there. My mother would often stay for a while, but my father practically never came. If he did, he stayed for two or three days, but not even that much.

Judit: It was too stifling for your father.

André: It must have been an extraordinary burden for him. We spent the other half of the summer each year in Austria.

Judit: Together at last, with your father and mother?

André: No, my father never spent the summer with us. It was only my mother and I staying with some friends, the Lukácses. There were very few people that my mother liked. She mainly liked people who were from "good" Calvinist families, that is, people "like us". She liked the catholic Lukács family anyway because the man was a pediatrician, so, as her only son, if I happened to fall ill, help was right there.

Judit: He represented safety.

André: Yes, he did. My father always went to London, saying, among other things, that he was developing himself professionally. That was partly true, but he was also surrounded by a fine group of people, for example, a psychoanalyst named Augusta Bonard, who later invited me to their house as well and from whom I received my first stuffed bear. So it was a complicated family. That is, I mean that it didn't simplify our lives with my father disappearing for a month at a time in the summers.

But we were still talking about my mother returning from London to Budapest, and I was born there, in this city on the Danube. If she hadn't come back, I would have become a British subject. Well, I missed that boat. At this point, I'd also add to the story that at the Korányi Clinic in the twenties – as I learned later, since we didn't talk about it at all at the time – nine out of ten doctors were Jewish. That is, my father was "the goy", the only one. As a consequence, I mostly played with the children of my father's colleagues. That's where my emotional ties to Budapest's liberal Jewry originate. In one of my first analyses, Paul Parin, who was also of Jewish descent, ventured to say – in a manner unbecoming of an analyst – that my relationship is contradictory because it's as if I'd been persecuted, too. Perhaps he didn't understand that that was, in fact, the problem of the survivor. To what did I owe my survival?

I realize that I am again taking distance from my mother at this point in my narrative. Perhaps it is more pleasant to think about my surrounding than to force myself to continue my story on the subject of my mother.

To Judit: *She was always faithful to me.... Without her, I would probably never have managed to live with any inner harmony later. I owe her a lot, but, despite that, in the apartment where I found the old photographs, I only found one picture of my mother and at least eight of my father. And that also characterizes his role in the family a bit. My mother needed distance; you might say, she had a phobic personality. She was quite a helpless person.*

I have a formative memory tied to my mother, which is part of the family myth, but I don't know if it's an actual memory of mine or if I just know about it from having heard it told and retold. I'd cry every night, saying, "Mommy, don't go out, at least not tonight." Clearly, I was experiencing separation anxiety before the age of two. And my mother told the story, tens of times throughout my life among various groups of people, that when Milli got there I didn't want to be with Mother as much anymore. Just imagine how it felt for a kid to hear that again and again. Milli represented a major change in my mother's life, since I stopped asking her not to leave me. It seems my mother found that story very amusing....

Figure 7: Dear Fräulein Milli and little André

Ludmilla Karl, whom we called Milli and for whom I invented the linguistically mixed pet name Millike, came from near Vienna and lived with my family as a nanny from when I was almost two to when I turned about eight or nine. She spoke Austrian German and only understood a few words of Hungarian. As expected, she was fulfilling the role of a real Austrian Fräulein.

Judit: You weren't even three yet when Milli came.

André: I was younger. I must have been one and a half to two years old.

Judit: And not much later, you weren't even four, when you got Uncle Teddy.

André: That's right. When you said that I had a relationship with my mother ... that's true, but what kind of a relationship is it if you are not really wanted, welcome...? My mother remained always reserved. As a result, my relationship with her, well, was mostly very reserved—maybe even phobic. When we were with other people, she always said what a terrific thing it was that after two or three weeks I'd gotten so used to Milli that I no longer wanted her to stay closely to me at home.

Judit: Reserved. The semantic field of that word is different in each person's lexicon. Would you say something more specific about that?

André: During my medical studies, for example, I had a very good friend, a boy from a farming background. I was at his place once, and then at his wedding, too, in the village of Alsónémeti, close to Budapest. They had a very pleasant, warm family atmosphere. I saw this warmth, and I realized that I was actually a "cold breed". Today it sounds funny, but at the time it seemed like an unexpected psychoanalytic insight, the essence of which was that my mother was, in reality, a very cold person. She was a Protestant woman, shy, and not inclined to closeness or physical contact. When I threw it in her face as an adolescent that I was a "cold breed," she responded with a joke, avoiding any discussion about it.

Judit: How did you experience her reserved nature? What couldn't you do with her that you would have liked to?

André: It seems that she didn't like to stay or to play with me. Maybe Milli was with me to make money, or God knows why, but I think by the end we'd really grown to love each other. Somehow, in a way, I also became a child of Milli's. My mother didn't know what to do with me. She didn't touch me in any way.

Moreover, she also saw that Milli was occupying me, and that, thank God, she didn't have to. Beyond that, she was always worried. Do you get that? So if I did anything, especially later when I started to be more independent—which of course is relative - in the center of the city, there was no major independence in middle-class families at the time - but on Orbánhegy, in a villa district, for example, I managed to achieve more independence. So when she didn't see me or couldn't control me, she grew extremely worried. I don't know, for example, whether she kissed me in the mornings, but I doubt it. I know that we were always together with the Lukácses—the family I've already mentioned—in Austria in the summers for about three weeks or a month. The Lukácses were a good, modest, middle-class Catholic family from Budapest. The husband was called Jóska, the wife Mária, the older son Jóska, the older daughter Mária, and the two younger ones, I think, were László and Judit. Judit was also my father's goddaughter. Mrs. Lukács always kissed her children all over in the morning, before lunch, and after lunch, so in the usual modest, middle-class way. I never had anything like that. I was certainly jealous.

I always admired my father, although I think we were never on the same wavelength, especially not as I grew up. I haven't profited enough from him – but I definitely need to talk about that some more.

As for my parents, I have to speak about their marriage. If we are to be honest, we have to say clearly that my parent's marriage was not harmonious: my mother came from a well-educated family with a very rigid moral code and a lot of shyness and coldness. Her family had very strong ties to tradition. Despite the fact that my grandfather on my mother's side had divorced in the early 1900s, I think, for my mother's family, her later husband, my father—this strange man, this doctor who had run away from Transylvania to Budapest --, was considered a "mésalliance" (an unsuitable match). And they looked down on him a bit. On his part, my father had an aversion to my mother's family. In the interests of full disclosure, I've found letters that revealed that when my father was making no money at all in Budapest – before he received the Rockefeller Grant – he was getting financial support in the form of lending from my mother's family as they considered him a man with a promising future. Although my parents were very different as people, I think they had a couple of good years together in London. London fit my mother's ideals, and there was widespread admiration for this country in Hungarian society at the time.

Figure 8: Father and son (Imre and André)

To Ernst: *My maternal grandfather was, and this is important, a Protestant in Transylvania. The Protestants were anti-Hapsburg, and wrongly believed to be protected by the great Protestant power. He was also a local politician in Transylvania. He had a subscription for the English "Times", and every day he got the current issue of the newspaper, 250 km east of Budapest; the postal service was really good. Although he read this paper, he had never talked a word of English with other people. He had learned it like Latin, and could only translate it, not speak it.*

By the way, he pronounced "Times" something like "tee mesh," as if he were reading the word in Hungarian. Once he was traveling to Szatmár County by train and reading his paper, when an Englishman started talking to him. My grandfather wrote down for him in English that he didn't understand what he was saying, the gentleman should also write down what he'd like, and then he could answer him. And so it happened, and by the time they had corre-

sponded in this way for about 200 miles, they ended up really talking to each other.

To Judit: So, London fit both my mother's desires and my father's interests – as well as his desires. After this experience, on their return, he got a job at Rókus, the prestigious hospital I mentioned earlier. By that time, he was the breadwinner. That's what I was born into, and it lasted for nine years. It was one of the best periods of my early life. The ten-room apartment on Deák Ferenc Street represented security. Everything looked as if it would stay the same forever. I couldn't imagine anything possibly changing at one point, but it did.

Figure 9: Dr. Imre Haynal at Hospital Rókus with his team

My father's sister was an opera singer. In the twenties, when my father came to Budapest, she started singing at the Berlin Opera. She married Teddy Mahler, of Gustav Mahler's family, who worked as a vocal coach and piano accompanist with the same opera. The Mahlers were Jews, so they left Berlin in 1933. They had the right idea that it wasn't the place for them anymore. They went to Paris for a few months, where, as German refugees, they were not received very well, so they came to Budapest. However, they didn't have an apartment there, so, since we had ten rooms, they stayed with us for a long time. I adored that man, Teddy Mahler, because, unlike my father, he was home all day long and played the piano for me. And, since he didn't speak a word of Hungarian, I also learned German from him. Similar to him, people will often remark that my German is Viennese German.

Then came 1938, and my parents were listening, distraught, to the screechings of a certain Adolph on a very rudimentary radio (my mother would shake visibly with every such event). The occasion for this particular speech was the Anschluss. I did not understand, or perhaps I did not wish to understand, that my uncle, Uncle Teddy, whom I loved and admired so deeply was somehow different than the rest of us. In fact, he was the one who had a greater influence on me than anyone else, and his Viennese culture—along with psychoanalysis later—had a decisive impact on me.

They found an apartment at No. 19 on what was then called Horthy Miklós Road but is named after Béla Bartók today. That building was attached to the St. Imre Catholic Residence Hall, and it is to the Catholics' credit that they managed to live there for such a long time without being denounced and persecuted: Aunt Elma—my father's sister—and her Jewish husband, Teddy, survived that horrible period. They were never reported by anyone, and they were left in peace. So it was a building full of decent people. Still, Elma and Teddy were so scared that they came back to live with us on Orbánhegy for a while, too.

Therefore, I grew up at the intersection of three cultures. When I was in primary school, I came home from catechism class and asked my mother, whom I loved so very much, to leave her heretical religion behind because I wouldn't like her to go to hell. Her unbridled laughter in dismissive response armed me forever against an uncritical and superficial way of thinking, and, what is more—and this is what I wish to gratefully acknowledge and emphasize—also against any form of fanaticism.

Transylvania Calls my Father

> To Judit: *When the northern part of Transylvania was annexed to Hungary again (in 1940), the Transylvanian blood in my father*

was immediately stirred. He was offered a full professorship in Kolozsvár (Cluj-Napoca in present-day Romania). Beyond that, he had a different, likewise political, problem at the hospital in Budapest. He had started to put the law into practice that stated that poor patients at Rókus Hospital had to be treated free of charge. It was "obvious" that in doing so he was yet again taking money out of the city's pockets. So he was having a tough time of it again, and he thought it would suit him just fine to go to Kolozsvár. My mother didn't go with him. She stayed in Budapest and, although they never asked for a divorce, they were practically separated from 1939 to 1946. That caused me a great deal of pain. The more or less warm nest disappeared. Sometimes, I went to my father's for a month—I even went to school there for a year later on. I was living at 5 Fürdő Street in Kolozsvár, and I really didn't like it. That was the second year of what was called high school then. So why didn't I like it? Partly because it seemed like a barbaric environment after the capital. Some of the kids mostly spoke Romanian, and I didn't understand a word of it. I had landed in an alien world and experienced fear and hostility. My first experience of this sort, brought on by emigration. They were different from the Budapest kids. They were also rougher; they fought a lot more. I just couldn't get used to that world. I was afraid.

A Mysterious "Illness"

To Judit: *Then came a year with quite a strange story. It all starts with the fact that I had a very pleasant doctor, who once said, "Kid, you have adolescent problems." And then he used a word for it, one which had no real substance: he said, "Kid, you've got an anomaly." My father declared that the doctors understood nothing about me, but he still put me to bed, where I was stuck for nine months (this was around 1943-1944) with an illness that they probably already suspected at the time was not even an illness but a symptom of adolescence tied to the development of the back. It's called orthostatic albuminuria. I can still see myself then: a "kid" in bed for nine months.*

Encounters with the Irrational: My Story

My father thought that the doctors in Budapest weren't good enough, so he kept me with him in Kolozsvár. I felt very much abandoned because he was running after patients all day and I was cooped up in the apartment. Finally, my father and mother decided to bring in a highly respected person, Dr. Petényi the pediatrician. That was at the beginning of the German occupation in 1944. Petényi got to Kolozsvár. He was a wonderful man. I cherish his memory in my heart to this day. He arrived, examined me, asked about two or three questions, and then didn't say a word. The whole family was waiting to see what would happen. Then he told my father to go have dinner with him that evening so they could discuss matters. In the end, Petényi said that I should go to him at the János Sanatorium, and then they'd see about the rest.

Judit: He helped to get you out of there?

André: Yes, that's it exactly. I was in the sanatorium for two weeks. Until then, I had to eat everything unsalted or with only a tiny measured amount of salt—and then he said I could use two packets of salt a day. It was all just a lot of medical hocus-pocus. I'm absolutely sure of that, though I never talked to him afterwards—despite the fact that I later became a student of his at the university as well. Neither of us ever brought up that story again. But suffice it to say that a few weeks later I got out of the sanatorium, and I went to stay in Budapest with my mother. My father carried on with his life in Kolozsvár.

Judit: It was only the two of you living in the apartment? No one else?

André: Here comes the important part of the story because that's what would have happened if we hadn't had the war and the German occupation.

Judit: Was this still the apartment on Deák Street?

André: No, by then, we had been living on Orbánhegy, since '41. You know, Calvinism has its own benefits: my mother had always put aside a little money from what my father had generously given her for the household without even counting it. Soon this had ac-

cumulated into so much money that my mother managed to buy a villa. Although half of it was covered by a loan, it still enabled us to buy a home of our own. That's partly why my mother didn't want to go to Transylvania. When my father left around '39 or '40, they had already started building the villa. Buying the villa was primarily my mother's doing. We moved over from our previous apartment, and that turned out to be a good idea because the building on Deák Ferenc Street was bombed, and none of the people living there at the time survived. The villa is still there on Orbánhegy.

Figure 10: Newly built house in Buda, 1940

All these historical events had a rather complicated personal background for me. My father became a full professor and the head of a clinic at the University of Kolozsvár in 1940. I stayed in Budapest with my mother. This was a de facto divorce, about which they never spoke. Today, I think, I must have been quite depressed for some time because I kept on thinking about which boarding school I could run away to. It was then that the idea of leaving was conceived in me, or perhaps it was even earlier, and accompanied me for a long time (up to the time I settled in Geneva). Probably, my response to the situation was that I became "sick." Evidently I was enmeshed in a family conflict, of which

Figure 11: André with puli dogs Bolhás and Füstös

that time I had some perception. I felt disturbed by but not really conscious of what was at stake. As an example, when I was asked at school about where my parents were living, I answered that my mother was in Budapest with me but "my father comes often from Kolozsvar." In retrospect, now, I know from a letter my mother wrote to her mother that she even considered divorcing. I didn't know this at the time. I stayed in Budapest with her, which I preferred (was it my Oedipus complex to be as close as possible to her in the absence of my father?), but in any case my father, alone in Kolozsvar, wouldn't have been able to take care of me. The "circumstances made it" (or, was it the unconscious irrational forces?) so that declaring me ill, bona fide, my father found a way to care for me in his own way from afar, even in eliminating, practically removing, my former caretaking doctor. The conflict between my parents was displaced to a conflict about my illness and my doctors and I remained a common object for their worries and caretaking. There were certainly other motives of which I was not aware.

I became the subject of debate between my parents. My father wanted to stick me in bed from the outset because he was convinced that I was sick. (Perhaps this was an unintentional punishment because my attachment to my school and to my buddies in Budapest played a role in my parents' decision resulting in a de facto separation, which was never declared.) Or did I unconsciously attempt to unite my parents around my sickbed, worrying over me? Particularly because "making it right"—restoration—has always been my role. Would this be an exaggeration? Is it conceivable that I could have been bedridden for months, the son of a physician, a professor of internal medicine, for nothing? Isn't the irrationality that we are trying to understand located precisely in a situation such as this? My mother sought immediate aid in releasing me and found an alliance in Géza Petényi. It was 1944, during the year of the German occupation, and Petényi, the most famous pediatrician in Budapest, had been declared an honorary Aryan—based on the Hitlerian principle of "I say who a Jew is". This highly cultured man, who also was part of Ferenczi's circle, "cured" me within a few weeks: he rid me of all my symptoms, then freed me and gave me back my quality of life—in Budapest. It was a blessing, which in retrospect, I felt could have been a symbolic gift from an admired Jewish man that reciprocated my and my family's human solidarity with his people....

My father must certainly have had a winning personality, personally, professionally, and politically. He was a good father in the sense that he often protected me (even against the traditionally pietistic[14] influence of

---

[14] I use a number of terms tied to religious traditions in my writings, but I must clarify that, except for one uncle, my immediate family had little religious inclinations. I use religious terms to signify a *tradition*. Among families there were many differences in Transylvania especially, but also in Budapest: there were happy-go-lucky traditional Catholics; believers and non-believers; puritanical, pietistic Calvinists; and Jews who had survived many ordeals.

my mother's family), but also someone who didn't really know what to do with me as a child. As a result, I "adopted" many father substitutes, for example, my uncle Teddy and later the fathers at the Catholic school that I attended for eight years.

As for what sort of illness I had, presumably we will never know. It was a kidney disease, they said, *glomerulonephritis* in Latin. Was it really that? At any rate, they kept me lying in bed for nine months—my only friend, who could console me, was Füstös, my tiny, black, Hungarian Shepherd Puli dog. Even when he walked out of the room in the morning, after spending the night with me, he took care to make sure that his claws didn't make any noise. I also passed my exams with flying colors during this period because I stayed, always, an obedient little boy.... Later, during my medical studies in Zurich, I would reach the potential hypothesis that I had never had a kidney disease but rather orthostatic albuminuria, which is a normal characteristic of that age group.

So, except for the one academic year I spent in Kolozsvár, I did my high school studies in Budapest. The elite schools at the time were mainly private institutions, and most of them run by religious communities. The school closest to our home was too right-wing for my father's taste, so I walked everyday over to the Buda side of the city to attend the Cistercian high school, which was run by a monk whose grandfather was a convert from Judaism. My father was appeased, yet the future proved him right.

Figure 12: St Imre high school in Buda

These studies geared me in a "humanistic" direction, as they called it at that time. We studied a number of languages—Latin, Ancient Greek, German, French, and later English or Italian—the teaching of literature, history, music, and art history was good; but there were no excellent mathematics (perhaps I also had no talent for it) or strong natural sciences... It became a home during eight years where many threads of long standing friendships, bounds of solidarity and life-long loyalty were interwoven. This excellent school gave me an invaluable protection during the terrible war years and after. To the only child I was, it gave a priceless society of my age and broke my isolation. These Cistercians were modern men with an exemplary courage and general ethical standards during years of various persecutions. When my father's security had become shaky, the director inquired about him regularly and assured me that he, himself, and the convent were praying for him. Not often in my life did I experience such a reassuring care and benevolence.

WAR AND OCCUPATION (1944-45)

> *Memory... is the diary that we all carry about with us.*
> OSCAR WILDE

In Budapest, our Jewish uncle was hiding in our home, and thus we enabled him to survive. At the same time, my father saved a number of persecuted people in the cellar of his Kolozsvar (Cluj) clinic for which he received a posthumous Yad Vashem award.[15] Áron Márton, the catholic Bishop of Gyulafehérvár (Alba Iulia in present-day Romania), warned the nuns working as nurses at the clinic that revealing the secret would be a mortal sin in exposing these "patients" to death. And this had its effect. No outsider knew of the people in hiding, and they escaped death. There are hundreds of stories about my father's courageous actions told by all kinds of people in Transylvania and Budapest. In Romanian-Transylvanian Kolozsvár, a street bears his

---

[15] Persons recognized as a "Righteous Among the Nations" are awarded a specially minted medal bearing their name, a certificate of honor, and the privilege of their names being added to the Wall of Honor in the Garden of the Righteous at Yad Vashem in Jerusalem.

Figure 13: My class in St Imre high school

name and memory still today.

It is difficult to write anything about the war years, not only because of the anguish and pain of the persecutions, and those later of the revolution of 1956, but also because so much has been published already about this period—or perhaps because I have read so much about it, indeed, better things than I would be able to write on this topic. And anyway, it would have to be 500 pages or nothing. Anyhow, Hungary was basically spared of major military interventions during the initial years of the war; not of all events, however, such as the threat of Yugoslavian bombings in 1941, and the tragic beginning of anti-Semitic persecutions and the deportations of apatrid Jews.[16]

The fact that my parents did not live together at the time did not make my life any easier, but the war, for our family, really started with

---

[16] At the end of June 1941, based on a decision by the *Hungarian* Council of Ministers (not by a German authority) with reference to indeterminate citizenship, several thousand people of Jewish descent were deported from the country in August *1941* (3 years before the military occupation of the country) and taken to Kamieniec Podolski (Kamjanec-Pogyilszkij) in western Ukraine, where they were slaughtered along with the locals: of the 26,300 victims, 12–15,000 might well have been Jews from Hungary.

the German occupation of Hungary on March 19, 1944. We knew that my father was registered on a "bad list,"[17] with 300 other intellectuals. In June, he was saved only by the political chaos (caused by a change of government) and, in October, by the early liberation by the Red Army in Transylvania, where he was still living and working at the time. I barely saw him during those years because he rarely came to Budapest, it was not safe for him to come frequently to this city—and I spent one year with him in all in Transylvania. Strange and apparently inexplicable events happened in my environment with ever increasing frequency. A couple arrived in Budapest unexpectedly with a letter from my father to put them up: Berci, who was obviously a deserter and God knows on what kind of mission (perhaps to stop a shipment of medical equipment to Germany), and his wife Julika, a wonderful, balanced peasant woman. They both lived with us for months until the husband, in the powerful grip of a fear that suddenly overcame him, decided to give himself up. He disappeared on a November morning and we never, ever saw him again or heard about him. I became very nostalgic, as he had played so well with me.

Poor Julika only dared to cry at night so others would not suspect anything, since the building manager—to whom my father made an apartment available in the house free of charge, naively thinking that this man, being a policeman, would ensure our safety, if required—slowly turned close to Arrow Cross (Hungarian Nazis) and poked around us more and more to find out what was happening in our home. With a friendly face, he told my mother that "all of these people" (who these people were, you can guess) "will hang."[18] Is it possible that Berci sacrificed himself for our sakes by disappearing?

Uncle Teddy stuck around until the end and stayed alive. I will never forget how after the war he said to me, a young boy—I might have been

---

[17] I am alluding to the different organizations of German Secret Services and Hungarian Nazi movements who kept notes about their archenemies in order to be able to act against these persons at any given moment.

[18] After the liberation, I met that Imre "No. 14" Horváth on the tram. Armbands change quickly; in 1948, Rákosi pardoned lesser Arrow Cross supporters and allowed them to enter the Communist Party.

15 or 16 years old at the time: "We have lost the war. German culture will never, ever be the same as it used to be" (we always talked to each other in German). It was an incredibly powerful pain for an Austrian Jew. He died not long afterwards, falling down a staircase in a ruined building. Was it suicide? Is this the irrational again?

This reminds me of a suicide, that of my best friend, Andris Kótai. He was a classmate, who, having returned from the ghetto, did not find anyone from his family and became, then, an adopted child. In 1956, he remained in Hungary while many of our peers and colleagues chose to leave the country in the face of Stalinist repression. When I learned that he had committed suicide I was 41 years old. Obviously Primo Levi[19] was not the only one among the survivors of the Holocaust who chose this exit.

After some lively years with friends in school and around me, in 1945, I suddenly found myself in a dead, desolate, empty, desert-like city. Of my 24 primary school classmates, only ten survived. My great red-haired rival, Zoli Rausch, no longer shined in humid fall afternoons, pretending to be an auto racer. What a tragedy—there is no sensible explanation, unless we perceive the irrational. It is more than frightening: the appropriate words are simply lacking....

Since our house was located between two front lines, ten of us (the Haynal family and neighbors taking refuge with us) hid in a small underground cellar where, thanks to my father's foresight, there were a toilet and a primitive washing facility at our disposal. We could even heat it with the remaining coal. For water, as the "only man" I had to retrieve it from a public water point that still functioned. Evidently going there and returning was dangerous, but possible during pauses in the exchanges of fire. Beans were our usual menu: three times a day, with their consequent production of intestinal gas. It was Christmas... We spent weeks in waiting: for what? For the house to fall apart under the impacts? For a real liberation, as in the freedom of movement, a different life—but would it be better or worse? The ten of us, *ferkelnd* together, were in total insecurity. No way out...

---

[19] Primo Levi (1919 –1987) was an Italian Jewish chemist, author of several books, and Holocaust survivor. He committed suicide on April 11, 1987.

Our house was quickly occupied by the Russians, who burned some of the furniture to keep warm. They ordered us to leave which, as it turned out later, was also a cautionary measure. We walked on foot in the snow-covered Buda hills in the middle of the night, pulling my grandmother in a wooden laundry trough. The neighbors joined us with their two children, also evacuated from our basement, as well as my diabetic uncle, Béla, and Julika, whom I've mentioned (Teddy was, by that time, in the liberated section of the city), and drifted from place to place until we found somewhere to live for a time—successfully.

Figure 14: André's only diary during the siege of Budapest

This is what I lived through during the post-war events that lasted for months: the evacuations of people from ruined buildings to streets full of dead bodies and debris; the screaming and crying of women as they were raped by the soldiers of the 'heroic Soviet army'; and then what came after the liberation—occupation. Incidentally, women soldiers were no less cruel than their male comrades. This was the only period when I was keeping a kind of journal. Still, I do not wish to revive the oppressive details precisely. This little notepad still exists as my good parents hid it. Decades later, one of them brought it to my exile in Geneva and thus I could preserve it. In fact, it also taught me a lesson about forgetting memories. I cannot reimagine the burial of cadavers even when I read it, baffled, without doubt penned with my own script, in my diary. I describe that I participated in it. There is no trace of this memory in my mind. However some souvenirs are still very fresh, although I don't find any record of them in my diary. I can see our dog appearing along the embankment behind our new "refuge"... he had made his way all by himself from our house (occupied by Soviet military), crossing hills and woods to join us, just what you would expect of a civilized dog expressing his loyalty toward his masters. Real friendship. He even took risks across dangerous areas. Between these two extreme examples emerge faded patches of memories of my grandmother's burial: the image of a protestant pastor, the presence of my uncle, the wall of a house and a garden. Was my mother pushing me to write this diary to an absent, non-designated addressee, my father in Kolozsvár? So that he might know how it had been for us, in case something happened to us…

In return for cleaning horses, I was able to get a hold of horsemeat from the Soviet soldiers (they were Tatars, and they were a lot more civilized than the Russians were). They shared their porridge and gave me—"for the young man"—more than they had taken for themselves. Common work, common food: solidarity.

On other occasions, using a stolen knife, I helped myself, alone, in the middle of the street, from the meat of dead horses. Survival instinct is all I experienced: a deep, almost irresistible force; no time to pause and think—Freud and his predecessors, foremost among them Darwin, were right. Irrational, isn't it?

Figure 15: Budapest in 1945: Bridge over the Danube

André E. Haynal

Figure 16: Budapest in 1945

Walking in the street, I carefully avoided treading on the cadavers that lay around as reminders of the most recent fights, but they didn't avoid me. Intermediaries of the army called me up to bury them. It was not my first encounter with death, but nevertheless a good lesson "against omnipotence" as psychoanalytic moralists call it.

What happened in the city was more than irrational. It was insanity itself. Red Army soldiers were capturing young men in the streets so that they could carry them off to Siberia on trains. Apparently, the army had reported too many prisoners of war, and the "prisoners" somehow had to be produced. Two of my cousins were thus taken among these young people: one of them was among the few who had deserted the Hungarian army, which was supposed to fight on the German side, and had gone over to the Titoist partisans in the forests of Bakony, after which he had to spend three years in Siberia anyway. He later wrote a book about this experience.[20] The other died of a starvation edema (which was not well enough known then in medical world) after he came back to Hungary. One of my fourteen-year-old classmates could thank dysentery (the Russians were extremely scared of this because of typhus) for being thrown off the train to Siberia in Bucharest.

I was fifteen years old when one day I was dragged off to do forced labor, "malinky robot" ("a little work!"). It was quite an acrobatic feat to

---

[20] "A lapitás iskolája" ("The school of survival"), by Miklos Domahidy.

push a wheelbarrow filled with heavy stones along a wooden board, without any handrails, 10 meters above the river in full swing and then empty it into the Danube brimming with ice blockswithout being drowned along with the contents before returning to make the trip again. This time the grey Danube was more like a fierce, menacing animal and not at all the *"schöne blaue Donau"* of the Austro-Hungarian folklore. Toward the end of the day, I suddenly noticed that there was a possible escape. Several people would, from time to time, bypass the exit guard and just go out. In a sudden movement (a follow-reflex?) I found myself grasping my wheelbarrow and with calm steps, I passed before the guard, not forgetting to salute him: *"dobre djeny."* After I turned the corner of the next building, I left my wheelbarrow and began to run. Would they shoot after me? No. I continued to run, out of breath, straight to the house of my aunt who lived close by. I spent the night there, a good night. Good work, good night, good sleep. With the determination of an overconfident adolescent (which was also bolstered by a personal sense of "almightiness"), I had escaped their labor camp.

I will not discuss in detail every adventure of this period. It was a kind of Chaplinesque world, or perhaps rather the world of the Soviet humorists Ilf and Petrov. (Although their writings were even published in the Party newspaper called Pravda, *"Truth"*(!), that didn't prevent them from being executed later for anti-soviet mentality.) Enormous uncertainty reigned throughout the city and country, which the Soviets first liberated, then occupied.

AFTER THE WAR—THE LEADEN YEARS

> *Totalitarian regimes proclaim: 'We know how to make you happy. You just have to follow our rules. However, if you disobey, we will regretfully have to eliminate you".*
> JEAN-FRANÇOIS REVEL
> QUOTED BY MATTHIEU RICARD

I will mention one episode: in August 1948 I prepared to be smuggled out of the country by boat via the Danube to Vienna with the aid of a

Zionist organization. The motivation was for me to have the opportunity to study abroad, in England if possible. My father came in contact with them through a colleague, Miklós Káldor. A worn brown suitcase was ready for the trip, and my mother was rather sad to see me go, as was I (though I couldn't show it). I didn't want to miss this opportunity, but the idea of leaving for an uncertain amount of time was painful. Would I be able to come back? The iron curtain was already under construction. My father assumed financial responsibility (he had some money abroad through patients whom he had treated in Hungary). At the last minute, the plan fell through and I stayed in Budapest under the Rákosi regime, "the great Comrade Stalin's best Hungarian student," as he called himself. We were "marching towards a bright and wonderful future." The former Gestapo center on Andrássy Road was transformed into the ÁVO headquarters.[21] Deportation started yet again, most of the time, organized by the same people. Those who had earlier gathered the Jews were now attempting to destroy the 'grand bourgeois' (who often happened to be the same people), not to mention the well-to-do peasants who were now called *kulaks*, to use the Russian expression. There were many fresh developments on the horizon with the help of these old experts in torture...

> To Judit: *You asked me what kind of memories I had. I have nothing documented from that period at all; my father burned all the documents in the fireplace. The only memory I have left is fear. One of these was burning documents beginning in 1940–41.*
>
> Judit: *Why that in particular?*
>
> André: *I have no idea. One of the reasons might be that Ernő Gerő the communist leader was a patient of my father's. Gerő always*

---

[21] The ÁVO was the state security apparatus for the police and was established in 1946. Originally, its activities focused on defending the state and investigating "war crimes and crimes against the people," but soon the scope was expanded to the clandestine collection of information on those opposed to the communist political leaders and the system, creating false evidence for show trials. This came to light through the files, which were accessible during the 1956 Revolution.

came to the villa and not to the consulting room on Galamb Street—he was the only one for whom my father made that exception. And when Gerő came to the villa, there were three cars, not one. Men occupied the yard and came into the hallway, while my father examined Gerő in his own room. Meanwhile, the people accompanying him were sitting by the door and standing under the window.

Judit: What did Gerő seem like to you?

André: I never saw him. I was locked upstairs, but I knew what was happening downstairs.

Judit: Weren't you granted permission to move around?

André: No, I wasn't. But it was through Gerő that I also came to know this strange fear, the one that sets in when people come all of a sudden and occupy the yard and house, as if the area were under imminent threat. Later, it turned out that Imre Nagy had also been a patient of my father's at the time, but that had been considered a major medical secret then. My father was also one of the invited guests at Nagy's 50th birthday party (as I learned later from published material).

The chief of the Communist Party, Rákosi, was never a patient of his. And I heard rumors and legends that my father was supposedly taken to Stalin, but I don't think that was true. Although he traveled to Moscow once on invitation, I don't think he saw Stalin. There are a number of reasons why I don't believe he did. On the other hand, Imre Nagy was indeed a patient of his, and so was József Révai, the cultural dictator of the day. As regards Révai, my father was outraged about a specific matter: he had gone to see Révai at the hospital on Kútvölgyi Road, where the man happened to be reading Joseph and His Brothers by Thomas Mann in German. So my father asked him how that was possible and why he had forbidden the novel to be translated into Hungarian anyway. Révai replied that it was "not right for our people". Very upset, my father thought that it was not since the Middle Ages that there had *been a time when certain people were allowed to read a book and others weren't.*

Judit: So that means that your father sometimes talked to you about those strange and dangerous times?

André: No, only later in Switzerland: he visited me twice. I saw him twice after 1956, and after that I came to Budapest for his funeral. It was during a visit to Switzerland that he talked about the past.

There was another tale, which I think was true, unfortunately, and shows that, though my father was brave, he was also sometimes in somewhat of a state of disarray. When they were re-organizing the Academy in 1950–51 and holding receptions, Kodály and others were frequently in attendance, with a glass of wine in their hands…. At one of these occasions, Rákosi said to someone so that my father could hear it, too: "That Haynal doesn't like us." So my father said to the person across from him, "After what they've done, we're supposed to like them, too?" And it really happened like that because a number of people told me about it at the time and said I should talk to my father about keeping his mouth shut.

Judit: Yes, but in your father's understanding, decency…

André: …this went beyond that. I think he must have lost his self-control.

Judit: The way I see it, that kind of outspokenness was part of who your father was.

André: Yes, it was. So it was possible for dissenters to express their views, too, but we knew that the next meeting of dissenters would be at the detention center. By the way, you may be aware of how much patients cling to their doctors, and sometimes rightfully so, like Ernő Gerő.[22] At some point after '56, he lived on Pagony Street,

---

[22] Ernő Gerő (1898–1980), a Hungarian communist politician, a key figure in the communist dictatorship who held a variety of ministerial posts. Living in the Soviet Union until 1945, he was an NKVD (the former KGB) agent and sent to work in France, Belgium, Spain, and Portugal. He called the uprising a "counter-revolution", which was

which is not far from Sólyom Street. And you can guess who the old doctor was giving him injections every day, negotiating the 120 stairs between Sólyom and Fodor Streets.

The point is that that was one of the reasons he burned those documents because he was in serious danger with regard to Imre Nagy. The KGB wanted to know about the state of Nagy's health at all costs, and they wanted my father to write a report on it. But he replied that he'd taken the Hippocratic oath once and he wouldn't give any information about any of his patients to anyone. Someone, I think the minister of health, Anna Ratkó, said, "We'll see whether you will or not. We have ways of getting it." And then someone must have put a halt to the whole thing, but they were very angry that they hadn't found out anything. As a result, he ended up with a lot of patients who were members of the pyarty's upper echelon because they knew that he wouldn't betray them. That was kind of a vicious circle. He treated everyone except for Rákosi. Rákosi probably couldn't risk going to a non-communist doctor, and I think he was also too paranoid. In fact, he was probably the most paranoid of them all....

When I was a teenager, I came to know the prominent figures of Hungarian culture as my father's guests at our dinner table: Áron Tamási, who, in his autobiographical Ábel trilogy—Ábel in the Forest, Ábel in the Country, and Ábel in America—, wrote about the life of a Transylvanian immigrant and, in a gesture of friendship, integrated into another historical novel (Domestic Mirror: A Chronicle 1832–1853) the figure of my great-grandfather, József Haynal, and my Aunt Róza. Another friend of my father, the author Sándor Márai, became a closer friend of mine when I visited him during our later wanderings in southern Italy; unfortunately, I was unable to see him again in San Diego (California) before he passed away.

---

received by the population with considerable outrage. A few days later, he escaped to the Soviet Union, where he stayed until 1960, when he returned to Budapest. The restored communist regime headed by János Kádár did not permit him to regain power. He lived a secluded existence on Pagony Street close to my parent's house.

When I saw him near Naples, he asked me the question: "How do you [psychoanalysts] get them to tell you their secrets? People, you know, they don't like witnesses...." We talked about the problems, complications, and muddle of human relationship—in analysis and in life. This was one of my most unforgettable "supervisory experiences". The irrational appeared to me clearly; in the language of ancient mysticism: Spiritus flat ubi vult, that is, "The spirit blows where it will".

Student Life: Learning and Socializing

Life is not a problem to be solved, but a reality to be experienced.
Søren Kierkegaard

At the age of 18, despite having done well on my Matura exams, I was not mature enough to choose a vocation or career and their consequences. I would have liked to move in the direction of an independent profession—just like my physician father, but avoiding at all costs to imitate him—for example, as a journalist or a philosopher; thus being like, and not like, him. However, one could not make a living from the latter. Moreover, the shadow of the communism to come was already being cast over the country. The future, therefore, did not show great promise. Perhaps I was one of the last "free students" who was able to combine philosophy and psychology in his studies. I ended this adventure with a sort of comprehensive exam. After that, and thanks to a number of months working in a factory,—I ended up opting for the medical profession.

Studying captivated me. Without actually admitting it to myself at the time, I felt that I had chosen the right profession. On the one hand, I had to prove that despite being "a class alien" because of my background (with an intellectual father), I would be useful to the "country of workers and peasants"[23] as a good "specialist", while on the other hand I adored studying. Politics alternated between periods of repression (such as that of Rákosi) and those of "relief" (such as that of Imre Nagy in 1953, after the death of

---

[23] "peasants": those who endured and survived all the measures raised against them by the different iterations of those in power!

Figure 17: 1956: André in an anti-Soviet demonstration with students

Stalin). When ideological pressure was relaxed somewhat, I thought that I would follow my interest in psychiatry and the neurosciences, and when dealing with the psyche started to become too dangerously communist, I thought I would make a detour toward pediatrics.

Except for a few run-ins with the secret police (primarily due to my own silliness), passion and a compulsion to work actually put me in a very enthusiastic mood. Moreover, there were excellent options for entertainment even in those days in Budapest: opera, theatre etc. We decided to give up regular bridge games because it was not wise for five young men to get together regularly each week at the time (especially to play a 'bourgeois' game…).

How could I have foreseen that, when university students marched in protest from the statue of the Polish general Bem towards Parliament on October 23, 1956, over one hundred years after his death, that one result would be an incredible adventure for me? That December, I would find myself, fully unprepared, first in Vienna, and then in Zurich!

But, before that, within a few days of the protest, half of Budapest was again destroyed. Soviet tanks were brought out against some youthful Hungarian idealists, the "new liberation" by the members of the popular uprising was transformed into a major proper military operation, including the destruction of anything left that was still somewhat unshaken or surviving. So we, the medical students, "stole" some city busses (with the complicity of the drivers of the union's strike guard) to transport the wounded from the overcrowded hospitals in the centre of the city to ones in Buda where there was still some "room". Crossing the bridges over the Danube was not simple: At the military Soviet checkpoint, I was "asked" to leave the bus and stand against the wall (not an idea that I liked) and they assured me that they would only execute me if they found arms in the bus. Whether any one of these foolish young revolutionaries still kept some arms in their pockets or not, who could know? Not I, in any case. But our "liberators," satisfied that their work was accomplished, that all these young people would certainly remain invalid for duration of their lives, let us go. An appointment with possible death cancelled, yet again. Moreover, one of my dear student colleagues, Marika, whose body was riddled with bullets, and who would require a number of surgical interventions over a period of 18 months in the hospital, began her "treatment" in the bus to Buda.

During the upheaval, I was first elected a member of the revolutionary committee of medical students just completing their hospital practicum—what's more, with votes from communists, too. At the time, just as in many other cases, I ended up being the most tolerated person in the others' camp: I was an accepted non-Jew among middle-class Jews in Budapest, Catholic in a Calvinist family on my mother's side, and a Transylvanian kid in a Budapest high school. The "other group" always accepted me relatively well. They might have intuited some kind of tolerance, an ability to mediate or an inclination in that direction, acquired in my childhood in trying to keep peace between my parents; I added the occasional skepticism or even cynicism. I learned my lesson on anti-fanaticism early on, and I hope that I will never forget it.

There is No Great Future Here for Me

> *Life is never fair, and perhaps it is a good thing for most of us that it is not.*
> Oscar Wilde

In November 1956, after the crushing of the October's popular uprising (the third battle for Budapest; the first being against the Germans, the second against the oppressive and tyrannical Bolshevik Stalinist Rákosi regime, and now this one against the "cleansing" by the reoccupying Soviet army), a former classmate in an ominous leather jacket (which was reserved for ÁVO agents—KGB-related men were the only ones who wore leather jackets...) came looking for me on two separate occasions in the hospital. At that time, during war or revolutionary times, 6 or 7 o'clock in the evening was already considered late. His name may have been Kakuk (which is "cuckoo" in English; it was certainly some kind of bird's name), and he wanted to talk to me about what had been happening on the students' revolutionary committee (he had previously been a member of ÁVO). I quickly realized that they wanted to understand what was going on so that later, when the regime regained strength, they could decide what should happen to those who had played some kind of role in the events. Despite the fact that I wasn't looking for this revolutionary post for myself—I wasn't "ranting"—, I also wasn't convinced that things were taking the right course and whether it could be sustained against the Soviets or not, so I was skeptical. Anyhow, the fact remained that my name must have appeared in the documents, and this man looked for me twice. I was lucky not to be in the hospital both times, but these visits clearly indicated that the case of the revolutionary committee was not considered closed and now there were scores to settle and retribution to serve. And that's what happened. Two out of the five students on the committee stayed in the country and were later imprisoned. Three of us disappeared abroad and managed to start new lives. With this, a new phase started in my life, accompanied by a series of coincidences (or, irrationality?), luck, and adventure yet again.

Travelling itself involved all of these things. The train left the Eastern Station in Budapest, but we never knew how far it would go or, especially, what kind of checks would be imposed on the passenger by the power structure, which had slowly started to re-organize itself. The first time I got off in Győr, halfway to the Austrian border, but because I did not find a place to spend the night, I came back to Budapest—although not to the hospital, but to one of my aunts'. The next day I tried my luck again, and in Győr I had the great idea of going to the hospital there, since medical students from my year were serving their practice year in various hospitals in the country. I found a well-meaning classmate, who gave me a place to sleep on a hard examination bed in the x-ray room, hoping I would not be discovered there during the night—but, if I was, "we'll see what we can do."

Luckily, there was no emergency, although the 7 o'clock train to Sopron did not end up departing until 9 o'clock. I was reading a novel by Somerset Maugham entitled *The Razor's Edge* as passionately as I could, hoping that once we arrived in the border area I would not run into a checkpoint with my ID for Budapest. They would check IDs at the exit, and anyone without the right kind would immediately be loaded onto a truck and told that the rest would be discussed later.... There was an internment camp in Győr awaiting those attempting to escape. I knew Sopron because after I graduated from high school I visited one of my uncles there (who was later put in a prison camp to remove him from the border zone).

To Judit: *I remembered that before the train rolled into the station, it would cross a bridge, where it would slow down. I said to myself, if I were a sensible person, I would throw myself off the train and onto the dyke. And I did. I had to find my way down from the dyke, and under the bridge there was a road and then a little later I was already on a street. I was just walking along the street. Later it turned out that there was a check at the train station and they probably would have caught me.*

"Learning from experience" (Bion, 1962)—learning from my experience in Győr, I immediately went to the hospital.

To Judit: *It was posted that the physician on duty was György (Gyurka) Tóth, a former schoolmate. I found him in the duty room—he was shaving. He looked in the mirror, and, without turning around, he said, "You, too?" Sopron was in a border zone, where you needed a special ID, so nobody went there unless he wanted to get out of the country. Gyurka asked me whether I had any money because they had found someone who could get them across and I could join them, but I had to pay. Another classmate popped out from behind a curtain, a friend of Gyurka's, who had been waiting there for a day.*

All three of us got into an ambulance in the evening, which was a great help because ambulances were rarely checked. We lay down in the ambulance. We barely dared to breathe; after some 20 kilometers, we got out and went into a house. I felt then how lucky it was that Gyurka Tóth had arranged this. It was November 30, St. Andrew's Day. It was just like something out of a novel.

But in the house the woman there got hysterical, saying that we should go back home because her husband, Palika, had promised her not to go again, so it started with a big drama. The husband said that he wasn't going to take us but would explain where we should cross. I should add that at the end of November—I don't know how well you know that timeline of events—the Soviets closed that part of the Hungarian-Austrian border zone. After December 10, you couldn't really get out there. That was one of the last days. We knew that the Soviets were already there. If they were to have found three doctors with IDs from Budapest in a house at the border, there would have been trouble. But where could we have gone? Then this individual started to say that the amount of money that had been set wouldn't actually be enough after all. In other words, he was blackmailing us. I don't know to this day whether the woman's hysteria was real or not, whether the man had really sworn to his wife to stop, or whether they were just making it all up. So it wasn't like when we get to Café Gerbeaud and are asked, "May I take your order?" No, he said he wouldn't take us all the way to the border but would show us the way. And that's how it continued in this vein. We had to stay quiet during the trip. We got to a place, I still don't know exactly where—I haven't taken that route since then—so I don't know what the route would have been under optimal circumstances and how far the man would have taken us. We practically left all our money with him. At one point, he stopped and said, "Do you see that there? That's the border. So you go all the way to there. Then you turn right. And then when the rooster crows three times...." And so on. It was pitch dark. So he left us there, in a thick forest, with the encouragement saying that it would be all right! There are moments when you have no real choice. You either turn back, or break down, or go on. Of course, we went on. We didn't know where there might be landmines, and we didn't have any information about anything. We tried to follow each other.

A mass of reconnaissance flares, or Stalin candles, were not a gesture of generosity on the part of the Red Army (so that we could find our way better). They used them to insure that the glorious oppressor could surely find us with their bullets....

To Judit: *When they light up the night, Soviet soldiers shoot at everything that moves. So it wasn't exactly the greatest night of my life. But they didn't shoot at us. In that particular situation, in that border zone, however, I felt no fear, strangely enough, and I was convinced that we'd get through...*

A few hours later we caught sight of the lights in a nicely lit village, there were no such strong lights in Hungary any more. We carefully approached a sign: "Deutschkreuz"![24]

But it was still fairly distant, we didn't know if there were ditches with icy water in between or other obstacles between our destination and us. We didn't know how much we could stand up, straighten up, and move on, or if we might need to crawl. Finally, we got to the road ... the lit road! It was still before sunrise, and we didn't dare stand up because we were scared that they might see us from the other side and shoot across the border. We didn't know how much the Soviets would keep to the fact that we were already in Austria.

---

[24] Deutschkreuz, or Sopronkeresztúr in Hungarian (Németkeresztúr before 1899), was a market town in the Austrian province of Burgenland. (The father of later British psychoanalyst Melanie Klein practiced medicine there in the late nineteenth century.)

Terra Firma after Directionless Navigation

The popes later introduced the custom of kissing the earth on arriving in a country. If I had been familiar with this custom, I surely would not have missed the chance to do so. I would have done it with all my heart.

> To Judit: *We finally got to the village and were received by young Austrians who were friendly and kind. That great welcome might have been due to the fact that, in that part of the country, Burgenland, there were a lot of people of Hungarian descent and also that previously, until the Austrian Independence Treaty of 1955, it had been part of the Soviet zone and Soviet troops had only recently left that region. Those Austrians remembered very clearly what Soviet occupation meant.*
>
> *Judit: You enjoyed their compassion.*
>
> *André: We really were received with true solidarity. I fell asleep on a haystack in a huge building. It might have been a large stable or barn. That was another permanent feature of my life: that I was able to sleep well in every situation. I slept until 11 the next day, when my friends kicked me awake—yes, that's the proper expression—demanding what I was thinking. We got some soup for breakfast, and they asked us what was next. We didn't know. We were thinking that if we told them we had no money, they would put us in a camp. One of us said that the most educated person in the village would be the priest, but the three of us belonged to three different religions and we didn't know which clergyman to go to. The other educated person would be the physician.*
>
> *We decided to go to the physician, introduce ourselves, and tell him we were medical students. He was incredibly helpful. He said, "Look, you'll do two things. First, you'll take a bath"—and we took a bath at his place. "Second, I'll give you money for the train or bus, and you'll go to Vienna." I had a number of addresses in Vienna; we all had addresses. I later returned that money to him, when I sent him a book and a letter of gratitude. He was a very decent man. All*

in all—if it can be said—everything worked out very well. We were helped by coincidences and by people…

We were not short of adventure later, either. In Vienna we arrived as gentlemen (and not as comrades!). The waiting room at the train station was heated, even though it was considered second-class. (In Budapest, that kind of thing had long fallen out of practice.) The following day I looked up an acquaintance of my father's, a merchant of tea and "colonial goods", who had given refuge to his entire family from Budapest and, so, could only offer me a place to sleep in the bathtub. Since he had to get up early for his business, this situation was not really convenient. I had to find another solution. But before I continue the story, I would like to remember the kindness and understanding of the Viennese and to express my immense gratitude to them. It's true that Vienna had also been a city of the Third Reich. After a decade of harsh occupation by the Soviet military authorities, colored by kidnappings (they had often used ether to put Hungarian escapees to sleep and carried them back to Hungary on boats on the Danube), the Viennese knew well what Soviet occupation meant… (see the British film The Third Man).

Onward: Preparation

Per aspera ad astra
(Through roughness to the stars)
Latin Proverb

I spent the days on the trams—it was free for us refugees to take them and they were heated, so I found a shelter there against the icy winds blowing through the streets—and I know some of the tramlines in Vienna even today quite well. Of course, there was something to do every day because I went to an embassy every day to see if they had an open spot in their country. The key moments of the story, however, demonstrate all the way to the present day how tiny coincidences (the work of the Irrational!) may trigger important decisions. Walking along one of the avenues, I happened to run across one of my colleagues (a medical student from Budapest), who greeted me in a thoroughly smart outfit, coiffed hair and manicure, and a big smile. Her name was Etelka Ferenczi—a family name (no relation with the psychoanalyst Sandor who would play a major role in my life later on)—and she was in good spirits and well dressed. What was up with her? She invited me for a cup of coffee—she had money, but where from?—and told me that she was working for a refugee organization, that they had a list that might contain the names of 1000 candidates to be admitted to Switzerland, and that she might be able to get me on the list. Who knew I might be travelling to Switzerland shortly after that? Altogether, I had a briefcase with a book and a few sheets of paper and my grade book, for which I had broken into the registrar's office at the medical school with a passkey earlier, on me. My original plan—to immigrate to the United States with references from relatives there (my mother's older sister Lilly and her family) or perhaps to Canada—vanished in the air in a minute (it was not an attractive prospect to spend the nights in a bathtub for months). Whether I liked it or not: somehow I would remain a 'European'.[25] However, for quite a long time I did not give up the possibility of immigrating overseas; perhaps, as a continuation of this, my children were born in the U.S. later, and my daughter today lives in the U.S. When I think of my daughter, I'm reminded of the concept of the family unconscious. If such a thing exists, then the question also arises of the signs that would mediate it—some of which are nonverbal—, is this part of the irrationality?

The series of coincidences, the irrational, has been present and recognizable continuously. The train carrying the refugees would have left for Neuchâtel/Neuenburg, but because of a case of typhus, at the last minute, we ended up at the La Pontaise military base in Lausanne. The date was December 6, 1956. Since everything relied on spontaneity, it took a while for the thick-walled, damp military building to warm up a little bit.

To Judit: *It was very cold. The base in Lausanne is on a hillside.*

---

[25] Rather unwillingly, since I don't have confidence in the future of Europe with its outdated nationalisms, ideological limitations, and with Russia at our backs.

The huge French Alps range is across the lake there. Those mountains evoked horrible feelings in me at that time: the feeling of yet again being locked up. Impassable mountains towered before me, and I was no highlander. I was an urbanite. The view soon brought out all of my feelings of being locked up.

Perhaps this was more tied to my fantasies; I had just come safely out of an enduring trauma of being locked up and I was now allowed to feel its significance…

Judit: Did you think you were going to stay there, or did you consider your stay temporary?

André: At first, I didn't think anything. I really didn't know, but I saw that Switzerland was a good place to be and that I was lucky to have been permitted in. Three days later, I received a document saying that I was in the country legally. The Swiss arranged everything, and as soon as we received all our shots—because that was a requirement on the base, with everything being done the Swiss way, hygienically—I left the place, since I had an address to go to. It belonged to one of my father's friends, actually, someone in Manfréd Weiss's family; they had left during the war when Manfréd Weiss handed his factory over to the Germans in return for being taken to Switzerland or Portugal, and then it became a German factory until the Soviets got their hands on it after the war.… One of the Weiss daughters was married to Franz (Feri) Borbély, who was a doctor of Transylvanian origin in Budapest, a very old friend of my father's.

Judit: Does that mean that your father also supplied you with addresses in Switzerland?

André: He gave me one address there. Earlier, Borbély had also managed to get out—and became a professor in Zurich. So I had their address. In those days, I didn't speak French as well as I did German.

However, in a children's home, I made a little money as a Romanian-French interpreter. Luckily, the children spoke a little Hungarian, and the caretakers a little German. This is how I was able to earn a couple of francs so that I could get to Zurich and register at the university to complete my medical studies. In Zurich, everything was a lot more organized because of the Swiss-German efficiency, and there was also an agreement as to how many students they would take on. Those who were able to complete their studies quickly enjoyed an advantage. I had all of my gradebooks on me. There were four of us in the same situation. They immediately took us on, and Péter Szondi, Lipót Szondi's son,—a future lecturer at the University of Berlin, who later committed suicide—translated all of my grade books and certified the translations. In Hungary, I was almost done with my exams, and I had only "important" subjects missing, such as Forensic Medicine and Marxism-Leninism (although I was probably one of the very few who, for example, read Engels with interest) along with some other insignificant subjects. In Zurich, I was obliged to repeat six semesters and take all—that is, all 24—clinical exams again. If I add it all up, I have taken the medical exams in my life in four different situations: as a medical student in Hungary, as a foreigner in Zurich, later as a candidate for immigration at the Canadian embassy and finally as a Swiss citizen in Geneva.

Zurich

In Zurich, a German-speaking region, there were few who willingly wished to deal with genetic research (family trees) ten years after the war. This academic field, with much of its literature in German, was replete with racist elements. However, it was an ideal job for making some money as a part-timer concurrently with university studies. *L'appétit vient en mangeant,* or "The appetite grows while eating;" that is, everything that we delve into becomes interesting and the English-language literature on genetics, which I studied initially, seemed exciting. A new period started yet again. I'm grateful to this day to Professor Urs W. Schnyder—later dean at Heidelberg University Medical Faculty—for giving me this opportunity. And I did what one could do for this job. I did not have amazing results, but they probably did not expect me to. During this period, I had time to read a lot of literature, as well, with the intent of polishing my German: Thomas Mann, Bertold Brecht, Erich Kästner, and the Viennese, for example, Stefan Zweig and Franz Werfel. Naturally I had a professional interest in literary texts as well, since I profited from it in the first place for psychology not for medicine (incidentally, I was already attending the Szondi Institute's teaching programs). I heard about cybernetics for the first time at the Swiss Technical University (ETH)—I became very excited and wanted to stop my medical curriculum to study cybernetics. Not only did my friends try to hold me back from pursuing it further, so did my weak math skills. Who knows how different my life would have been if I had given in to my great enthusiasm and ended up finding myself among the pioneers of computer science?

Judit: You've mentioned that you had gotten married.

André: In this inner state and situation, in 1958, I suddenly married one of my former girlfriends—or rather in '59? I went to analysis after that. It wasn't a very good idea to get married before the analysis. We got divorced one or two years later. She went to Canada and now lives part of the time in Canada and part of the time in Zurich.

Judit: Was that about what Imre Hermann called "clinging to each other"?

André: Yes, it was. But I realized that the relationship wasn't the "clinging" that I was looking for.

Judit: Well, obviously, at the time, each of you needed the other.

André: Yes, but not anymore later on.

Judit: I guess that was accompanied by a great deal of tension.

André: A lot. If I could have a new edition of my life, I wouldn't do it.

Encounters with the Irrational: My Story

EUPHORIA WAS GRADUALLY REPLACED BY THE DOLDRUMS

Man – a being in search of meaning.
PLATO

I felt depressed because of a feeling of longing for my friends in Budapest; I was getting depressed about the stolen dreams that I had conceived in the city of my birth, about a beautiful future there, and probably many other feelings as well that I couldn't specify or explain at the time. In the meantime, I received my medical degree, I earned my M.D. and I found my first real job at a small hospital in the northern part of the Zurich canton, in Bülach. I was enthused that I was able to practice general medicine in its entirety. As there were only two house physicians for all of the departments, we were on duty every other night. As compensation, we were allowed to eat from the hospital cafeteria, - preferably within a few minutes. Part of our program included, naturally, the occasional baby delivery at night. I would tell all my friends with pride that I could even work as ship's physician. Ship physicians at the time had to be able to do surgical interventions, if necessary, since there were no helicopters available for rapid transportation. I really liked the slightly maniacal atmosphere.

André: However, it wasn't easy after that environment to land in the country town of Bülach. So I didn't give up my apartment in Zurich, and I had to buy a used VW.

Judit: A VW bug?

André: That's right. I commuted about 12 miles every day there and back. Except for the days and nights when I was on duty, I wouldn't stay in the village. I'd enjoy being in the city.

Judit: The village oppressed you.

André: The village and isolation. I'd left behind a very intense life in Budapest, which I had lived and loved between 1948 and 1956. I'm telling you about it because perhaps it's these changes that prompted me to begin a psychoanalysis. I experienced a lot of anxiety, for example when I only had 30 Swiss francs left for the last week of the month and it wasn't enough. I had far more anxiety over that than over crossing the border. I started getting seriously depressed in my abandonment, in my nostalgia, and in my homesickness. It was not a homesickness that would take me east but back in time. It didn't mean that I wanted to go home to Budapest or to my parents. I missed the company and the friends—in fact, my past way of life that I was suddenly torn from. I started experiencing depression, which encouraged me to make the decision to begin an analysis, and soon that's what I did.

Judit: Do you remember the signs that pointed to your depression?

André: It is important that you ask what the "symptoms" of my depression were in Zurich. I was, from time to time, very sad. I felt a kind of nostalgia. Many of us have felt something like that. I was longing for a better life than the one I had experienced until then. I didn't see any way to attain it and to realize my dreams. I needed analysis for that. That was the main motif of my analysis.

So as I was in that very small hospital in Bülach I realized that my degree from 1960 was only sufficient to work as a junior doctor for 732 francs a month—that's how I started out. As mentioned, I was on duty every other night. I was locked up every other Saturday and Sunday, during which time I was the only doctor at the hospital. So it was impossible for me to go out to the garden to listen to the birds chirping. When it became clear to me that that was how it would always be, I said to myself that I would try to get a specialization. And if this degree of mine were acknowledged on the North American continent, then I would go there soon. I even went to the Canadian embassy, where I was able to take exams identical to the Swiss ones. They were difficult and challenging, due to the language. A man read out a case history and even put his pipe in his mouth to make sure his English was even less comprehensible. We had to analyze a text that was read out quickly, a psychosomatic case history of which I understood only half.

Judit: What sort of a psychosomatic case?

André: Well, it concerned a woman with a general medical problem. I think everything was all right with her, except that nothing was all right. Nevertheless, I got the necessary Canadian recognition. That was a piece of paper—some kind of an entry document—that could be used for some years to travel to Canada, get a first job, and then take the real exams.

I got it. But I didn't go to Canada. Although that was one of my options in case I couldn't make it in Switzerland. And then what we call "chance" had a hand yet again.

While I was working at that small Bülach hospital, I signed up for the university neurological clinic, where I was told that they would have an opening in five years or so! I said to myself, "I either go to Canada or I don't know what I'm going to do." But what should I do for five years in such a difficult job with no prospects? This was not my calling. Then, in April, a secretary called me: if I could come immediately, the job was mine. I went to my boss at the hospital in Bülach and told him that I was terribly sorry but I'd been asked to go to Zurich to the neurological clinic at the university. People at the time were very fair in Switzerland: my boss said that one "should be selfish" in such situations and advised me to accept the position. It was only a few months after he had taught me how to practice in that hospital environment. As I had been considered a

Figure 18: André and the University Neurological Clinic, Zurich

reliable person, my leaving was not good news for him. Now, he had to look for another assistant for his little nest, which did not pay very well.

Judit: Why did you choose neurology?

André: Why did I go into neurology? I was convinced at the time—and I'm actually still convinced of it today—that what happens within us happens in our brains, and I don't think that I was mistaken about that.

Judit: What attracted you to neurology? Your father was an internist, and your grandfather was a pediatrician and head of a hospital.

André: Neurology as it appeared in Hungary in its complexity was a more intellectual area than my father's profession, internal medicine. That attracted me. On the other hand, I was also able to do something different from what my father and grandfather had done—something that I considered more sensible and better, based on my views at the time, something that I placed on a higher level.

Judit: So where did you end up then?

André: At the University's neurological clinic in Zurich, after those nine months in Bülach.

Thus I started neurology at the same time as I started my personal psychoanalysis. At the clinic, I didn't have to report that there'd be regular absences due to my psychoanalytic sessions.

Judit: They wouldn't have looked on that favorably?

André: They didn't look on it favorably, although I slowly realized that a number of important people—among others, a cadre, if I can put it that way—were also undergoing analysis. There were pretense, conformism, and behavior that were hostile to Freudianism. But I wanted to go to Freudian analysis. Moreover, everyone advised me that if I were to go to America it would be advantageous to undergo analysis with someone who was recognized internationally. In contrast, if, for example, you engaged in Daseinsanalyse, they might say that that's a German and Heideggerian invention, *maybe even Nazi. Since I was on duty every other night, while I was living in Bülach, it was not feasible for me to go to analysis at the time. When I started working in neurology in Zurich, I could also start analysis with a doctor called Paul Parin, who, strangely, ended up becoming some kind of a Marxist-Freudian later on in the 1970s and engaged in deviant activities in Zurich, which was frowned upon in the international organizations.*

When I went to him, everyone recommended him highly, even the Borbély circle. He was one of the big names, so to speak. Later, I realized that Franz Borbély had also undergone analysis. He went to Szondi. That was interesting, since I was also in contact with Szondi.

To Ernst: *Already one of my professors at my school in Budapest had been interested in Szondi and the Szondi test. After the maturity (the university entrance qualification) this contributed to the fact that I chose to study philosophy and literature. This was in 1948, and this choice was actually a very bad one, because that was the time when the Communist party was slowly seizing power. This was the end of psychology, and also of Szondi, and there remained only Pavlovianism. In exceptional cases it was still possible to lend Szondi's notes from the library for a specific work, but they were restricted for other people. So it was a bad choice. I pursued those studies for nearly three years, and focused mainly on the history of philosophy, and did only a bit of psychology. Psychology was more and more "reduced". So I realized that there was no future in this, and then I seized the occasion when it became possible for me to switch to medicine, which was really something quite extraordinary at the time. It surely helped that my father was a university professor. In any case, my interest in so-called depth-psychology started with Szondi. In Zurich, too, I began to study at the Szondi Institute at first. This seemed not to be the right group for me, however, since I saw that the more intelligent and bright people were in the Freudian group. But my encounters with Szondi himself were interesting. I was perceived as a Hungarian refugee at the time, and so he invited me to* his place, mostly for Sunday mornings. In fact he invited me to come and have an "apéritif" with him, but then we talked about all kind of things, about Kant and whatever—a real Budapest talk. He switched from Kant to the Nazis, and from the Nazis to depth psychology as he saw it, and so on and on. He was a very intelligent and highly cultured man. He had two children. Tragically, his son, Peter, committed suicide after having become professor of German cultural history in Berlin, I believe at the Freie Universität. The daughter was a psychiatrist in Zurich, who worked mainly in forensic medicine. Although he did invite me to an apéritif, he never really offered one, only much apple juice, which I didn't like so much, I'd have preferred orange juice ... He particularly impressed me with his humanistic attitude. He had been interned in Bergen-Belsen, and had founded a Humanistenbund [Humanistic Association] in that concentration camp. He made a great impression on me; he was a wise and serene man. He made interesting remarks that I partly did not understand at the time...

To Judit: *So Szondi was a very special person, the way everyone is special. For example, I said that I would be going to Parin for analysis, which he could well have frowned upon, being an analyst himself. "Good for you," he said. "Good choice, he is a recognized man, and you need to move on." Szondi was struggling with fairly great difficulties. He never received a license to practice medicine in Switzerland and was only able to work as a psychoanalyst, not a physician. Previously, in Budapest, he'd been the director of a psychology laboratory and had an M.D. He also knew the complications of life well, and he very much recommended that I take the route that appeared to be the safer one. So I went to Parin, and I didn't regret it. I underwent intensive analysis, sometimes even six sessions a week. Things were done differently then. We agreed on my going four times a week, but then it turned out that it would be good for me to go on Saturdays as well...*

So how did I get into psychoanalysis in Zurich sometimes even five or six times a week? Well, this is part of the true story about finding my satisfactory inner balance. When I was young, years before, I tried meditation under the influence of a book about Tibetan Buddhist monks who worked miracles and then a book on meditation by a Catholic literary celebrity Ottokár Prohászka (whom we can see as a kind of forerunner to Teilhard de Chardin).[26] I had also toyed with the idea of following such a path, and it was actually truly on my mind for quite some time. Among other motivations, I was also driven by the desire to get away from home, to be liberated from an oppressive paternal authority and a family home filled with conflicts. I achieved that, but forcibly—is that part of the Irrational again? In Budapest, family tradition, a housing shortage, and financial dependence on one's parents left minimal options, or perhaps none. In Zurich and Bülach, I was able to experience the opposite: I was free—but alone. My friends and girlfriends were able to ease this only for moments. But that time I had been interested in psychology (and literature), which was also influenced by the remnants of psychoanalysis that existed in Budapest up to 1949. I was primarily studying Szondi with great enthusiasm - what an irrational preparation to being a regular visitor in his house as one of the representatives of "depth psychology" in Zurich! His books in Budapest survived even the ghetto[27] only to meet a worse fate in the 50s: they were placed on a list of works that could not be borrowed from the libraries (the only permitted psychology consisted of descriptions of the Soviet Pavlov's experiments with dogs—that was it... Perhaps this reflected how these "specialists" saw their own society. as an experiment of conditioning by orders and consecutive punishments). In the name of Marxism-Leninism, the regime decided that "depth psychology" did not exist any longer and the works in this discipline should no longer be borrowed from the libraries. One of my friends, László Luka, who dared to want to borrow a Freud

---

[26] Ottokár Prohászka (1858–1927), attempted to integrate Catholic and modern ways of thinking in the early twentieth century, prompting the Vatican to place some of his works on the Index. His political "positions" are largely controversial (like his support of Horthy regime and what he called "a-Semitism").

[27] After the war, he found himself in Zurich and continued his life there, together with his family.

volume was taken for interrogation and questioned about "what purpose" for which he wished to read it. Later, he was imprisoned for such "similar" behavior until 1956, when his colleagues, myself included among them, remembered his being locked in prison. We demanded that he be freed and the way to the West was opened up for him then as well. By some irrational link I met him again in Zurich "by chance" and again later in Geneva by surprise and our friendship of over 70 years flows without any conscious effort to keep its wonderful continuity in life over all these years… He became my daughter's godfather.

Psychology was overshadowed at the University of Zurich by late German phenomenology. The turn came about with a young *Privatdozent*, Ulrich Moser, who at the time was Szondian but later became a famous creative Freudian psychoanalyst….

2

Depression and Creativity

The Meaning of Despair

> *O Melancholy, be not wroth with me*
> *That I this pen should point to praise thee only....*
> NIETZSCHE

I was up to my neck in psychoanalysis in order to rid myself, once and for all, of the doldrums and their alternative euphoric exaltation. The study of depression interested me even after this for a long time. When, in 1976, at the *Congrès des Psychanalystes de langue française* (the Congress of French-speaking psychoanalysts), I was asked to be the keynote speaker, I chose this topic. It was considered the first detailed psychoanalytic study in French to deal with depression.

> To Ernst: *The reason for this was that the French-speaking analysts found—I did not agree—that Freud had not given his best in "Mourning and Melancholia" (1916-17g), and that the psychoanalytic literature on depression was quite meager, consisting of only a few quotations, mostly from Freud. In short, it was not a favorite subject, no "showcase" topic. Why this was so, is something I discovered only later: probably because it had been the Kleinians who had written about depression! When I gave my manuscript to*

Madame Spira, she told me: Of course I am very much for it, after all I'm a Kleinian! So in choosing that topic I crossed some faction border.

In my lecture, I tried to assess the literature, almost as if soliciting the "aid" of all psychoanalysts who formerly had devoted their time to study this problem. My text was published later as a book in French as well as in English; I chose as the title: *Le sens du désespoir* [The Meaning of Despair] or *Depression and Creativity* (Haynal, 1985).

There, following Freud, I called attention most prominently to the parallel between the processes of mourning and that of depression. For example, often *guilt*, either well founded or not, hides behind depression—the feeling that we have missed something we didn't do that we should or could have done. I think that one aspect of analysis itself is a process of mourning. Because of the sad connotation of this aspect, it is often underemphasized or even suppressed. Moreover, others, primarily in France, were of the opinion—perhaps because of a latent anti-Kleinian[28] attitude—that mourning is not a psychoanalytic category.

I believe that all the great psychoanalytic thinkers after Freud, for example, Klein, Winnicott, Bion have been mending holes: they noticed what Freud hadn't thought of or hadn't thought through as extensively. In my understanding, works by other psychoanalysts most often are supplements, the expressions of points of views rather than counter-arguments nullifying views or facts that were presented before. In this context psychoanalysts have often difficulties with *innovation* : it seems to bring them in a conflict between a truth already acquired i.e. an important insight, and another idea taking a different direction. This arouses the fear of abandoning, even destroying the validity of insights already gained. However, it is just the moment to examine whether the two visions are really contradictory or are compatible, whether they could both exist according to the

---

[28] Melanie Klein was a Austro-Hungarian born psychoanalyst who studied intensively the depressive states in children and adults; she was fraught with controversies, especially in France, because of her innovative views.

point of view or the context. That is the complexity of possible relationships between the old and the new.

The way my depressive feelings described, in the first circle of this work, found expression, and my research for possible reasons for it—as well as an unconscious mentation on it in a second step-- lead to the working through in my analysis and in my inner (personal and cultural) work thereafter furnishing the foundation of my book *Depression and Creativity* (1985). The core was born out of some feelings and self-perceptions that gave fruit to a mental elaboration later.

The questions we asked ourselves at the outset were: Does despair have any meaning? Is it a particular phenomenon, or do we find it in the lives of us all? Since any developmental process is, of necessity, accompanied by external change and the loss of successive inner states, is not despair a necessary concomitant of human development? Certain of its aspects are brought out through the mourning that takes places during psychoanalysis, when our erroneous representations of the world and of oneself are finally relinquished.

I have attempted to investigate the problem of depression using the concept of *trauma* as a starting point. For various reasons, this concept became very controversial in the history of psychoanalysis. It was feared that using it as the primary lens through which to understand human life would hide other eminently inner problems. There was also the question of knowing whether or not early sexual seduction and abuse is an important factor in disturbing the normal evolution, as Freud saw it at the beginning of his work. Ferenczi showed later that trauma is more or less omnipresent in human life, in the form of difficult situations in which the early ego is overwhelmed. Freud, in his late work, as in his essay on Moses (1939a) expressed the view that traumatism is a universal phenomenon. A long defeat in the face of consequences of traumatism with a feeling of helplessness is a frequent path to depression. Ferenczi and others later underlined as well the multiplicity of traumatism, which thus becomes a repetitive element of life. Not all frustrations become trauma, as we may have the necessary ego strength to overcome some of them. In my view, trauma can be conceived as an inadequacy, as the gap between an external event and the subject's capacity to work it through. Understanding the mourning process gives us some indication as to the unfolding of the psychoanalytic process; both are the gradual working through of something traumatizing, that is, something that could not be overcome earlier, in a less mature stage. As the early development blossoms, and the success of the child's efforts at separation - individuation (in Mahler's sense of the term) becomes an important factor in reinforcing his/her narcissistic security. This leads us to the problem of loss and change as depression-generating elements on the basis of a particular narcissistic vulnerability. A loss sets in motion the internalization process, whose particular nature will be brought to light in depression. Fear of change is, in the final reflection, a separation anxiety vis-à-vis particular states or what we call "objects" of our emotional interests, like present or past persons of our life. The questions that remain are: how narcissistic vulnerability can lead to massive introjections; why persons suffering from separation anxiety are unable to bear losses; and why the loss of infantile omnipotence probably lies at the root of all these losses.

If we take into account Freud's experiences and his thinking about the Oedipus complex which he considered the core of all neuroses, it is in this complex, that the subject can gain narcissistic satisfactions as well as pleasures coming from others, called "objects," which, in turn, gives them their importance. The upsurge of interest in depressive and narcissistic phenomena in recent years is perhaps related to changing parental roles and their consequences on the younger generation. In some cultures, the decline of the traditional parental protective and repressive attitudes of the parents appears to have resulted in otherwise structured - or differently designed - superegos in their children.

The progressive individuation of a child in a normal development installs the additional elements of the self going beyond "reparation" and opening opportunities to construct new horizons like inventions, art, etc.

Where do the *new* elements of creativity come from? This is one of the central questions I am interested in. Creativity often follows a loss - this gives us a good hint! Depression is the mourning of this loss and after this first phase comes the "reparation", as a second phase. This restitution of what was damaged is the source of the energy found in the act of creation.

In these reflections, I try to show how many threads are interwoven all along our life in the interminable repetitive movements of *loss, reparation,* and *creation*. Through this process we reach adaptation and we are lead, even further, to create. Freud, as already mentioned, posited this whole problem in the framework of what he called the "Oedipus complex", i.e. in an interplay between three persons where the third one imposes frustration and loss of satisfactions, of sorts. For Freud, narcissistic vulnerability comes from the fact that the baby lost the satisfaction tied to the assistance and care of the mother in a conflict with the third person (often the father). New rethinking of this evolution by the group following Melanie Klein and the representatives of the baby-research school show that all these problems have their roots in very early periods of life. Later separations then touch the already-present sensitivities...

My life and the elaboration I attempted in my own case illustrate how a simple perception of loss can be thought over through an array of associations, a working through, a new creative endeavor such as writing or another cultural production.

In children, the narcissistic wound, springing from helplessness and sexual immaturity, is more open, more exposed, since less repressive Oedipal taboos manifest the child's incapacity and immaturity (experienced as a narcissistic wound) more clearly.

While the liberation of the sexual content has ceased to occupy a center stage in contemporary psychoanalysis (Green, 1995), it is now the inner contradictions engendered by the sexual content on the one hand, and the internalized prohibitions and ideals on the other, that determine the perturbations, feelings of insecurity, and depression apt to bring the subject to psychoanalysis. Analysis consists in the quest for a better tolerance of tensions, an attempt at integration in spite of dissociative tendencies. Its ultimate aim is to provide a sense of confidence within the context of the prevailing and inevitable insecurity that is life.

Within this perspective, the most fundamental question of psychoanalysis is not, in my opinion, the "myth of origins" but rather, the "origin of evil," evil here viewed as the disruption of inner equilibrium, the source of suffering, uneasiness, anxiety, and psychic pain - in short, what has been termed "frustration." For Freudians, absence, frustration (Rapaport, 1967), and "lack" (Donnet and Green, 1973) are present in rudimentary form even at the origin of thought itself.

The enigma of evil, lack, and frustration imposes on the human psyche the never-ending task of reappraising. For Melanie Klein, it is related to the "death instinct," the threat against life. According to classical theory, it is prohibition, the appearance of the Law, that is responsible for these experiences of unpleasure as a frustration of the instincts predominates. This great change condenses all frustrations in order to constitute the human personality, thus presenting itself as a prerequisite of psychological development. The world's great religions brought together the suffering of moral obligation and the obligation of asceticism, of expiation. In so doing, they perhaps expressed the sense that this suffering is bound to the Law.

Freud showed that knowledge and understanding go hand in hand, and that the obstacle, the stumbling block of the problem of evil, can be overcome by understanding. If the individual is to be spared the vicious cycle arising from a perpetual sense of injustice (the injustice, as in the "bad" of the Other, or the sense of oneself being "bad"), it's inevitability, and eventual resignation to it, human life must be, with all its clash of truth and error, good and bad, accepted as such. Depression, on the other hand, implies a resigned retreat in the face of this obstacle. Analysis encompasses the problem that lies at the heart of the depression by attempting to elucidate it, while at the same time combating any tendency toward bitter resignation.

Camus (1942) proposed to consider the matter of suicide as one of the most important questions of philosophy. Is life worth living or not? Would suicide be an adequate response?

> To Ernst: *The first sentence in his book on Sisyphus reads: "There is only one really serious problem in philosophy: suicide." And the last: "We have to imagine Sisyphus as a happy man." So we have to roll our stone again and again to the top, but at least it is <u>our</u> stone.*

All the ideas around these questions touch our thinking, our thoughts about depression.

Psychoanalysis has shown us that we must be able to live in the shadow of despair. Our demons can be neither expelled nor stifled: they are precious to us as an attribute of human existence. If we learn how to live with them, they will even end up helping us, in the sense of promoting a psychic equilibrium that might be called a "eudaemonistic moral." Traces of our losses and despairs, born of the child's primary condition, his helplessness, will accompany us always: in the words of Seneca, "The Fates lead the willing, and drag the unwilling."

It is latent despair and the feeling that one's inner world is crumbling that finally incite the subject to a working through, with all its pain and toil, thus paving the way for a better integration of the inner world and opening to innovation. This work can be accomplished outside of psychoanalysis as well, through the cultural process; success in either is creativity.

3

The Guidance of the Irrational

"Transfer" (Über-tragung)

During my time in Zurich, I dealt with neurology for four years. Moreover, I also spent one year in neurosurgery. The fact that our impulses and emotions are embedded in our bodies was often on my mind. In Switzerland, as in the U.S., it was a custom to separate neurology, psychiatry, and psychotherapy as distinct disciplines. I was probably the only person, or one of the last, to study all of these (formerly, Freud could also have been a similar example, but at that time psychoanalysis was just in the making and not established as a separate discourse). I first underwent psychoanalytic training in Zurich from 1960 to 1964, in parallel with my personal analysis with Parin. I was really in need of this, at the very least to rid myself of the unwanted root sprouts of my personality, but also because I was suffering from chronic or hidden depression accompanied by slightly hypomanic and—it can be said, successful—social and sexual compensations. I also realized that the sources of creative ability might open up for me in the process. As my analyst noted, "Don't complain, because the sensitivity you gain here makes it possible for you to earn a living." This seemed to be no small consolation for me; moreover it revealed the complex truth about the patterns of the irrational in my choice of a therapy and, simultaneously, a profession.

To Judit: *André: I deeply believe in what we call coincidences, but I don't know what "coincidences" really are. I still went to Parin, with whom I believe I underwent very good analysis for years. Then, once I went to an evening performance of a cabaret artist from Vienna, Georg Kreisler, who was a known poet, composer, and singer. That genre didn't really exist in Hungary in that form, but it was popular in Paris, Vienna, and elsewhere. He wrote beautiful poems or, rarely, but sometimes, borrowed them from others, and then sang them. I had a record on which he was laughing, and then I was suddenly shocked: "That's Parin!" He had the same laugh and the same accent: Viennese. I hadn't noticed it for years—after having heard Viennese German since I was three (from my Uncle Teddy, Fräulein Milli, and others) and not having learned any other kind of German as a child. As it turned out, somehow everyone knew it but me. They also knew that the Parins were a family from Tessin, who had migrated to Slovenia through Trieste and, when the war was approaching, Paul Parin went to study at Graz and then returned to Switzerland. He started to focus on neurology and psychoanalysis in Zurich.*

Judit: So you had a similar background.

André: That truly came to light after the analysis. I told him a number of times that he can't understand anything what I am telling because he doesn't know Hungary and in the end it turned out that his grandmother was a Hungarian Jew from Budapest. Amazing how one chooses one's analyst! My unconscious attention may have noticed the accent in particular (but my conscious attention did not) as I had a major interest in linguistics at the time, particularly in German dialects. Having already spoken Viennese German in my childhood and having picked up some elements of Yiddish in Central Europe, I later learned Swiss German and 'Hochdeutsch' (standard German), which I spoke well and wrote particularly well. (I might note, parenthetically, that when I was writing forensic reports, I was asked where I got my excellent style. "You write better than the German-speaking Swiss," one of my bosses said enviously.)

To sum up, despite it all, I wasn't consciously aware that my analyst had a Viennese accent.

Judit: Did you discuss that with Parin sometime later?

André: In a later step, at the end of the analysis. In the period after my analysis, Parin also published a book about his own life, a kind of novella, so I learned some more details about his life. He must be around ninety now.[29] The phone book says that he's a Schriftsteller, that is, a writer (and not a psychoanalyst any more). But to finish the anecdote, yes, Parin was an important stage, my first analysis.

PSYCHOANALYSIS IN ZURICH

> *You can never tell with bees.*
> WINNIE-THE-POOH

Psychoanalysis in Zurich at the time was multifaceted and stimulating. I was surrounded by a number of fascinating people: Fritz Morgenthaler and Goldy Parin-Matthey participated in Paul Parin's travels and ethnopsychoanalytic research in Africa; Jacques Berna represented child analysis; Harold Lincke was interested in the complexities of ethology, then an emerging field; moreover, Gustav Bally was drawn to anthropology; and Martha Eicke dealt with the relationships between psychiatry and psychoanalysis—just to mention a few scholars among those with whom I had personal contact. Even Medard Boss, a *daseinsanalyst*, was part of the Society and ran his own institute.

To Ernst: *There was a leading group of analysts, all of them personalities with the most diverse interests, and together they formed a formidable group. They always met in the Odeon Café, I think on Friday evenings...*

Ernst: *... the café to which also Lenin went?*

---

[29] At the time of this interview, Paul Parin was 89 years old.

André: Yes, exactly. The premises of the Institute were in Kirchgasse, only a house or two from where Lenin had lived. But the point is that there was that coffeehouse culture, in contrast to later psychoanalysis, above all in Britain or America, where analysts did not show themselves in public like this. One could say that this Zurich group was more "exhibitionist". Everybody could see them or approach them. This was a different, a much more open culture, which actually reminded me very pleasantly of what went on in the circle around Ferenczi in Budapest, if we believe the reports. So these were interesting people, who had many animated discussions, but had also very personal ties, where for instance the wife of one analyst married the other one… This did not have much in common with the later professionalized American institutes.

And I also had a supervision with Morgenthaler, who had a very fickle temperament, which frustrated me on more than one occasion, especially as I was expecting an evaluation of my work. In a given moment, he could say that I impressed him by knowing everything about psychoanalysis: "How do you know that…? Of course, you are Hungarian" (which I didn't like hearing because I did not want to be identified as an alien). Another time again, he said: "They say you are a fairly good neurologist, why do you insist on becoming a psychoanalyst?" His belief that I would soon return to Hungary convinced me that he did not want to understand anything about my situation. Today, I think that it was much less a kind of Olympian indifference but rather a denial of Soviet realities widespread among certain salon leftist intellectuals. My other supervision in Zurich with Arno von Blarer was marked by extraordinary intuitiveness, and helped to make balanced continuous work possible and pleasurable.

My basic psychoanalytic training in Zurich proceeded from the late-Freudian model, focused on the Oedipus complex in men, and was characterized primarily by dealing with the problems of the superego.

To Ernst: *In hindsight, I find that at the time the Zurichers were kind of disoriented. I remember that Fritz Morgenthaler told me one day, with his usual impulsivity, that he would have to call Rudolph Loewenstein on the phone concerning a problem that came up in my supervision, so that he could see what he, Loewenstein, thought about it. A phone call to New York! At that time! In other words, outside of France there was a feeling among analysts around the world that the intellectual leadership was to be found in the New York kind of ego psychology. That ego psychology, however, contributed very little to revive psychoanalysis after the war. It was mainly concerned with analyses of defence mechanisms. There existed a kind of axis between New York (and the Yale group) and London, the New York group and Anna Freud's group, and this was perceived as "true" psychoanalysis. But the "truth" was in fact an analysis of defenses. Naturally this is also something that concerns psychoanalysis, but one no longer loved the unconscious. The unconscious was actually perceived as psychotic, and was not loved.*

An earlier paper of mine, written about the ego-strength, carries the hallmarks of this period. At the time, the explanation for each thought and action that did not fit the superego was punctuated by: "Why not?" With the enormous external influence of the youth movement of '68, there was a straight path leading directly to the desire to abolish all regulations, guidelines, and social obligations… "Why not?"

To Ernst: *The dominant model in psychoanalysis at the time was Freud's model of repression, and in general one wanted to be freed from repressions, and particularly of super-ego repressions. An analysand would say, for example: "I masturbated", or: "Hey, I won't pay any taxes to this corrupt state", and the analyst would answer: "Ok, why not?" It was a question of the analyst's permission. This might be debatable, but may I, as an analyst, permit or not permit, that is, forbid? Can I simply say: You are entitled to follow your impulses without repressions or inhibitions? When for instance the analysand says: "I copped a feel on that girl's breasts", and the (female) analyst would answer: "Ok, why not"? We then made fun of the fact the she, as a feminist analyst, should never have been able to say that. In groups, there exist crystallized stereotyped interpretations. You notice it when in a discussion someone says something stereotypical that came from his group. He also wants to be liked by his group, and to show his solidarity; even in a mixed group he is loyal to it. Group realities and group ideologies are played out and used to play off others.*

The conflict that developed within the psychoanalytic society was pre-programmed by such *enactments*. The colorful and interesting group of older members (most of them were about 50) did not feel at ease in this blocked situation of which they were trying to stay ultimately in control; they found new ideological support in an overenthusiastic reception of Kohut's ideas about narcissism (this ideology 'allowed' psychoanalysts also to be narcissistic). The followers of the younger movement then split off and organized their own seminar, with the support of some of the older analysts who joined them. For the latter ones, it was also rejuvenating. Enthusiasm for narcissism soon abated. A little later, I was the president of the Society and, at first, I was saddened by the developments, but then I thought that development, thanks to the stabilization of the group's identity could still be possible.

To Ernst: There were also colleagues, however, who suffered under the splits. Some people in Zurich sometimes call me the "Spaltungspräsident", that is, the president of the splits, someone who brought about splits; it is actually meant as a reproach. My conviction was, however, that splits are not necessarily something bad or evil, as with the split in England into three groups during World War II, when each group could thus develop an identity of its own. They were different, but they could talk to each other, because they were no longer at war, but co-existed. Let's leave out for the moment that the British temperament may have also contributed to bringing peace.

In France, there were not only the Lacanians, but also an intermediate group, between the APF, the Association Psychanalytique Française, standing for a French/intellectual renewal, the group around Lagache, and the SPP, the Société Psychanalytique de Paris. The three groups were clearly defined, and the people were in a much better position to know what was offered or also what was out of the way for them. Instead of chaos, there was a certain possibility of orientation. I thought that something like this could also happen in Zurich, so that the Freudomarxist group, on the one hand, and the traditional group, on the other, could live better with one another if they weren't forced to wage war in meetings until two o'clock in the morning when everybody would be utterly exhausted, but instead could choose, in certain situations, between two organizational structures. This was not only my opinion, but a view we shared in many informal talks among others with Paul Parin, my former analyst, with whom I had maintained a friendly relationship. I believe we both wanted to bring about an amicable solution, instead of other options that were no longer possible. I did not regret this, even if there were losses on both sides, particularly older analysts who did not want to belong to either group, or went to both. I believe that this solution was a rather positive one for the society, and above all for the new members and the younger generation.

SEEKING A NEW LIFESTYLE. DISCOVERING GENEVA...

The world is a book, and those who do not travel read only a page.
AUGUSTINE

Gaudeamus igitur, Juvenes dum sumus
(Let's be joyous as long as we are young)
STUDENTS' SONG FROM THE MIDDLE AGES
LATIN PROVERB

Judit: What was your life like between 1960 and 1969, for almost a decade?

André: That's when different shades of lifestyles—sometimes called "alternative"—and corresponding relationships spread. I lived in Zurich for eight years, followed by two years in Lausanne and the rest in Geneva. I was at the polyclinic[30] in Lausanne from 1964 to 1966 because that was the only psychiatric polyclinic with a psychoanalytic inclination in Switzerland at the time. After that, as of 1966, I lived in Geneva.

Judit: Why did you leave Lausanne, the only polyclinic with a psychoanalytic orientation?

André: It was only possible to spend two years as a trainee there. Originally, I had wanted to return to Zurich, but there were job opportunities offered in Geneva, which changed my prospects. There was a change in the person of the "patron," as someone in that kind of position was called at the time, i.e., the head of a University's psychiatry department; a new director came from Paris, who, although he himself was not a psychoanalyst, wanted to introduce the psychoanalytic orientation as well. I got a better job, in teaching and training psychiatrists, since I was already a trained analyst as well as a neurologist and psychiatrist.

Judit: You wanted to go where you could practice psychoanalysis the most.

André: I was hesitating over whether to return to Zurich or not. The competition was very stiff there, and it wasn't easy for a foreigner to get a foot in the door. Jungians, Szondians, Daseinsanalysts, and Freudians were all in the running. I loved Zurich in spite of it all. It's the largest city in Switzerland, and the most interesting things happen there. For me, Lausanne was a tiny, rural nest, but with a very good polyclinic, where I was able to learn a lot with a great many patients who were in need of psychotherapy and psychoanalysis.

---

[30] Etymologically, policlinic means *polis* (city) *clinic* (place for care), according to the German spelling, but became, by misuse, polyclinic, which would mean a multiplicity of clinical departments, as it is spelled in contemporary English.

So after Lausanne, I moved to Geneva, where a person with my qualifications—who was at home with neurology, psychiatry, psychotherapy and was even dealing with psychoanalysis—was highly welcome.

To Ernst: *The situation was quite chaotic. Geneva was very different from the rest of Swiss psychiatry. It was an old-fashioned world. There was a man, Ferdinand Morel, who had been a pastor and had studied theology, and was inclined towards philosophy, but not in the sense of modern epistemology, but rather in the classical, Kantian sense. It is complicated to understand him… Many treated him badly; I did not, because I found that he stood for a specific situation. There was the old neuropathological psychiatry, and practically no psychoanalysis, in contrast to Piaget and Claparède at the institute of psychology at the university. In medical psychiatry psychoanalysis had never arrived. And I was the man who was familiar with both.*

To Judit: *The new director, Julian de Ajuriaguerra, was originally a neurologist and later became an analyticophile child psychiatrist.*

Figure 19: Prof. Julian de Ajuriaguerra in Geneva

André E. Haynal

Figure 20: Professor Julian de Ajuriaguerra dancing

To Ernst: *He had lived in Paris, and made friends in psychoanalytic circles. He also participated in the experiments with mescalin by Henri Michaux, a surrealistic poet. So he was himself a marginal person in marginal circles, and was surrounded by poets and painters who had been influenced by psychoanalysis. He came from the Basque country. His brother was politically active there during the Second World War, as a leftist, anti-Nazi politician, as well as in the Resistance in Paris.*

There was a big fuss and many difficulties when he was appointed professor in Geneva, you can't imagine ... One always says that academic quarrels are so virulent because the controversies are about petty matters, but here the matters were very important indeed. Some on the faculty favored a psychiatrist from Basel in German Switzerland who was perceived as a representative of the industry ...

Ernst: *... that is, of Big Pharma, of which Basel is a center ...*

André: *... and who was actually convinced that psychiatry would only progress by developing and using better drugs. Ajuriaguerra on the other hand was first and foremost a humanist. He had undergone psychoanalysis himself, even if he never trained as an analyst. He had analyzed with Sacha Nacht, a German name for a French psychiatrist and psychoanalyst of Romanian extraction, who was* *also president of the Société Psychanalytique de Paris, SPP. For the faculty in Geneva this was a very important decision, between a psychiatrist with a pronounced orientation towards psychopharmacology, and Ajuriaguerra, who had written four big books on the histological analysis of brain parts, and who had also applied psychoanalytically inspired methods and psychotherapies in the treatment of children...*

Ernst: *...and who was obviously a man of many talents. From self-experimentation to brain anatomy, from personal analysis to child psychotherapy, to relaxation therapies and to extramural psychiatry...*

André: *...yes, very stimulating. When he came, he first focused on child psychiatry and expanded an institution for that purpose. At the same time he opened the doors of the asylum and the clinic Bel-Air, the closed ward, which was felt by some as too much for a first step...*

Ernst: *Bel-Air is the Cantonal psychiatric clinic in a suburb of Geneva, the equivalent of the Burghölzli in Zurich.*

André: *And as in Zurich there was a connection to the university; the clinic directors have to be professors. The professors are appointed by the Faulty, a complicated, very Swiss story.*

To Judit: *I got to Geneva in 1966, and at the beginning of the seventies I was first promoted to Privatdozent and then in 1973 to professor. Until then, psychoanalysis was rather a Swiss German (Zurich and Basel) and Lausanne specialty. It had few representatives at the institutions in the rest of the country.*

The university accepted from Ajuriaguerra, this man with a winning persona, the idea that psychiatry should open its doors to the influence of psychoanalysis. Unlike the majority of the school of medicine in Geneva, he was a leftist thinker and, first and foremost, a non-conventional person.

Judit: *During those ten years, you were finding your way, and one important factor was obviously where you'd be able to stay for a longer time.*

André: And a period that was meant to be final, in spite of the two years I spent later in the U.S.

Judit: Yes, but that was transitory.

André: There was always a sort of restlessness in me, and so I thought of Geneva as final—until something "more final" would present itself.

This restlessness frequently underpins the unintended life of reluctant émigrés, as if the new place could neither be the same nor what is desired. Moreover, even if the emigration was felt once as a success, it can fuel the desire to try the next opportunity that might thrive even more (a wishful fantasy). Many tales describe this destiny, for example in the figure of the Wandering Jew condemned to eternal journeying.

Judit: After all, Geneva plays a significant role in your life.

André: It's become more than significant, it has become my identity.

Judit: Your second and third marriages are also connected to Geneva. Your second marriage brought a new emotional quality into your life.

André: I was always monogamous, that is, I was bound to one person, but in a sort of successive polygamy. I have the sense that my second marriage was very good, I lived very well with my wife, and if we'd had children, we probably would never have divorced. She already had three children, with whom we both actually had an excellent relationship. I remain on good terms, especially with the oldest son, who later became one of the directors of the International Red Cross. We're going to see each other now—just next week, I'm going to spend the weekend at his place in the mountains.

Judit: Your second wife was a physician and a psychoanalyst as well. Was she already an analyst when you got together?

André: When we met, she was in training, having divorced from her first husband, the children's father.

Judit: The one who died later?

André: Yes, that's right. Hers is an interesting life story. She grew up in Tunisia in a French and Italian family—her grandmother only spoke Italian—and then she received her M.D. in Paris at the Sorbonne. Then she came over to Switzerland, and it was very difficult at the time to make ends meet in Switzerland with a foreign medical degree. In order to overcome that, she registered at the department of psychology and got a degree in psychology with which she could conduct psychotherapy. And once she had both, she started her psychoanalytic training. When we got together, she was more or less done with her analysis.

Judit: Actually, it was before you two met that she had started on the path that later became your shared path—at least for a while.

André: Yes, and when we got divorced she returned to Paris.

Judit: You not only experienced what was missing from your earlier life in that relationship—the warmth, the devotion, the belonging together—but it seems that you also shared intellectual interests.

André: Yes, that's true.

Judit: So this ten-year-long relationship had a double cohesive power. You were already a practicing psychoanalyst at the time.

André: I was already a "full member" of the Swiss society then. All this happened between 1970 and 1980, while I was teaching at the university and also in charge of a clinic. I lived with my wife as of 1969, and we were divorced in the early eighties.

Judit: Going back to your profession, did your patients follow you to Geneva? That would have represented a safe transition.

André: The mentality in Switzerland was very much tied to the cantons. That's changed a lot by now, but in that period, for example, it meant that a teaching degree from Geneva wasn't accepted in Lausanne schools, or, for instance, the electrical plugs that worked in Zurich were no good in Lausanne and what worked in Lausanne was no good in Geneva. It's incredible but each canton was a statelet of its own, and each decided for itself what to accept and what to reject from electrical plugs to teaching degrees.

Judit: *This system actually made your settling more difficult. Your arrival in Geneva opened up a new phase in your life.*

André: *I relocated, that is, I adapted to a new situation.*

To Ernst: *I was shocked by the different stance of psychoanalysis in French Switzerland, particularly with regard to the relationship with France, which was completely different, for example, from the relationship the Zuricher group had to Germany. The Zurich group was quite autonomous, and might itself had a certain influence on the Germans, but not so much the other way around. Mitscherlich and others were ideologically close to some of the Zurichers, but, well, Zurich was Zurich in psychoanalysis. Some Germans did come to us, also Mitscherlich during the war, but not like in western Switzerland. Diatkine and Lebovici trained practically all the child analysts in Geneva and Lausanne, coming regularly to those places at least once a month, or even twice. One could also earn much more money in Switzerland than in France. But they had a kind of imperialistic attitude. For them, psychoanalysis was not Vienna or Zurich, so to speak, but Vienna and Paris, with Paris being the center of French-speaking psychoanalysis. This may be true. Of course, the center of French culture is Paris. The great discussions there, however, for instance around Lacan, how to read Freud, what Freud really wanted to say, what is psychoanalysis about in the first place—all those problems never came up in Zurich, at least not in a similar form. My contact with Paris was Jean Laplanche at the time. I wrote him a letter about the contemporary translations into French as I gave a seminar on those texts; I wrote him about what I saw as mistakes or problems. Then he answered in a patronizing way, to this insignificant Swiss who nagged about the German language… In fact, I had a good relationship with him later on, that's not the problem. He, Laplanche, was not really fluent in German, but he had his own opinion about psychoanalysis and the important statements in it, and what would differentiate him from*

Encounters with the Irrational: My Story

Lacan. Later, and this was decisive for me, I experienced a completely different atmosphere in London, above all with Balint, but also with others.

My beginnings in Geneva were an important but actually painful time for me. I had had my analysis with Parin in Zurich and then came to western Switzerland, and it felt like a slap in the face. In my naïveté I thought I would now be an "analyzed" person, with all the connotations of idealizations this term had at the time. The first whom I heard very critically question this term was Balint, by the way. I was a young man, I was an émigré, and I had already lost many friends and many reassuring things in leaving Hungary and coming to Zurich. In Budapest, I was a student with many friends, an interesting boy for the girls, and so. And then I went from Zurich to Geneva, and everything I had achieved and re-arranged there, so to speak, was suddenly no longer valid. What I said sounded very strange in their ears. In my first seminar I was forced to study Abraham who really bored me... It was a different world, and I wondered about my future in this place. This was the second time when I absolutely wanted to emigrate. I could not deal with those people. They were also arrogant, anointed by Paris, as it were, and they looked down upon me, on this provincial guy who had come from German Switzerland. This is after all many years after the war, but still, in the eyes of the Swiss Romands and the French-speaking psychoanalysts, German-speaking Switzerland had fed upon German books, and could not be taken quite seriously. Seriousness, that was the Paris culture after the war; that was Lévi-Strauss and structuralism; that was modernity and even already post-modernity, which emerged at that time, and post-existentialism, and everything that was exciting. And then there's you coming from Zurich and telling them that Sterba gave a beautiful talk in Zurich—that was really pitiful. I really asked myself if, in the eyes of those people, my whole analytical training of many years did not count for anything? It was really completely devalued. This was much less so the case in London. They always kept a respectful *distance and also incomprehension towards the French. They would say they didn't quite understand, but then they also weren't very interested. That was my impression.*

I had great difficulties in assimilating to the situation in Geneva. After all, I had to keep my head on my shoulders, and also my individuality, and my constitution let me keep them. I am a kind of pigheaded fellow, and have a certain continuity, a perseverance, and there were indeed also some interesting things, and so I tried to bring all that together. Still, with only a few exceptions, such as de Saussure and Marcelle Spira, my environment was not sympathetic.

To Judit: *Moving to the University of Geneva also meant a complete linguistic shift. My heart was aching at the thought of losing my German, which I had so mastered by that point that it was at a literary level, and I had to learn another language again, one I hardly knew.*

Judit: *How old were you when you started French?*

André: *I'd taken French on and off, first in high school and later privately, when I was attracted to literature, essayism and philosophy.*

Judit: *And what about Latin?*

André: *Latin was a compulsory subject in high school, but I could have replaced Greek with French. As of the age of fourteen, in high school, I was able to choose from among three languages: classical Greek, French, and Italian. I took French for two years. Then I entered into a delirium about my future studies in philosophy. But for that I would have had to take a "Matura" exam in Greek or take Greek at the university. I'd decided to stop taking French and opted for Greek. In two years, I had completed four years of material, and I ended up passing the Greek exam. I still remember the etymology of some of the Greek words. Later, I only used it to be able to register as a philosophy major. So I did have some knowledge of French, but the bulk of my learning came from the movies, French films, in Zurich. I think I've already mentioned that they didn't translate films at the time.*

Judit: Did they have subtitles?

André: Yes, they did, and I'd sit there every evening watching a French film. I'd watch the same film with subtitles three or four times a week, so my knowledge of French comes from films, if it seemed necessary, and great actors, such as Jean Gabin, Jeanne Moreau, and Lino Ventura. I had the grammatical basics, but I actually learned French at the movies. At the same time, I lost some of my German, and for a while I even forbade myself from subscribing to the "Neue Zürcher Zeitung," the best newspaper in Switzerland. So I had to make do with a lower-rate local paper in Geneva so that I wouldn't even have associations with German. These language shifts took up a lot of energy and cost me a lot. My strong proficiency in German disappeared. Although, if I'm in a German-speaking area—in Austria or in German-speaking Switzerland—after a good week, I can speak literary German again.

LEARNING, AND RE-LEARNING

It was through René Henny that I was able to experience the personality of a psychoanalyst at work. However, it was Raymond de Saussure who had the greatest impact on me. He was the embodiment of tolerance, balance, and, yes, wisdom as well. In one of our supervisions, he told me: "This woman has so many problems that you will never solve them. Except for one: her problem with you." That was his way of speaking about transference.

To Ernst: *De Saussure had his first analysis with Freud in Vienna, at the end of World War I, with which he was rather dissatisfied, and his second with Franz Alexander in Berlin in the 1920s, before Hitler.*

Then, fleeing Hitler, he first went to Paris around 1939 and worked as an *hypnotiseur* because that was the only professional activity he was allowed to practice there. He stayed in the French capital for one to two years.

Figure 21: Raymond de Saussure

Figure 22: Marcelle Spira

To Ernst: *He had his third analysis with Rudolph Loewenstein in New York. In a way he had made the same experiences I made, in different psychoanalytic cultures, and so we understood each other. It was like an unconscious capillarity, that is to say, we understood each other without ever addressing the topic explicitly. With one exception, maybe, when he invited me—and that was extremely unusual—to have dinner with him on the shore of Lake Geneva when I had become a young analyst. There he told me: You must study the history of psychoanalysis, there are several psychoanalyses, etc. This was my thinking exactly, and he sensed this. He was very intuitive, and confirmed this, as did Balint later. These were the two persons who greatly encouraged me to study the history of psychoanalysis, and since I came from the study of the history of philosophy, this naturally very much appealed to me.*

René Spitz also led a seminar in Geneva for several years.

He often apologized during his case seminars—"Pardon!"—whenever using technical terms. Free association was called for, not applied dogmatics.

To Ernst: *I think this shows the conflict I had in mind between using a schematic application of the theory and really listening to the patient.*

A later encounter was Marcelle Spira, the extraordinarily wise woman who introduced me to the Kleinian and Bionian world.

Figure 23: Marcelle Spira and Paul Parin discussing

To Ernst: *She was a Swiss Jewess who emigrated during the war to South America, I think to Argentina; she did not want to await Hitler's fate in Switzerland. After the war she came back, as did de Saussure, by the way. So there were two re-migrating Swiss with whom I finally found a contact and felt understood. Of the other influential analysts, some came from an intellectually, and hardly stimulating, environment.*

I had really had enormous luck with these persons, as they were able to further my personal development. Isn't that the actual purpose of any analytic activity?

Speaking of development, or, better put, catalysis, let me mention different experiences from two later personal analyses. One took place in Vienna, with a female analyst, Eva Laible, an Anna-Freudian, whose working style did not differ much from that of the, then, Zurich school of focusing the interpretations on the repressions of desired fantasies, ideas and emotions in conflict with the Super-ego. This analysis was very short and did not have a great impact on me.

To Judit: I've talked about the special atmosphere and the originality that prevailed in Zurich. But to sum up my first experiences in Geneva, I think that in Geneva my profession was suffering from the illness from which many other psychoanalytic institutes suffered: the old guard was convinced that they were the ones on the right path and whatever someone else thought differently must have been simply wrong. A kind of philosophical or religious school can evolve, where you have to know what to say or think. But that is not the right way to gain more inner freedom from the Freudian institutions. The possible recipe for avoiding difficulties to be accepted as member of the psychoanalytic Society consisted in going to "training analysis" with a highly prestigious Parisian psychoanalyst. I only realized that when I got to Geneva from Zurich, that they didn't believe in the same psychoanalysis as they did in Zurich. They even looked down on it. That was a surprise.

André: ...But it was a trial to go to Vienna from Geneva for analysis over the weekends.

Judit: Did that present a great deal of hardship and sacrifice?

André: It presented a major hardship and a great deal of work. There was never time to rest over the weekends because of the trip. And it was also difficult for her, too—although she accepted it, though I'm not sure if she was right or wrong to do so—for me to see her on Saturday and Sunday morning as well.

Later, in California, when I was 50, I underwent analysis a third time during my sabbatical year at Stanford, which then, four years later, led to another marriage. Suffice it to say, analysis, located in the center of my life as it is, represented a great experience.

Judit: Your first analysis was also in German.

André: The first two times were in German, the third in English.

Judit: None of them in your mother tongue.

André: Particularly during my analysis with Parin—I don't know whether it was out of intuition—I said, explained, translated a lot of things from Hungarian. Actually, Viennese German was a kind of second mother tongue for me. As I mentioned before, I've spoken it since I was three.

Freud supported the method of regularly (episodically) repeated analysis, but this advice was rarely followed in psychoanalytic societies; the blame falls on the complexities of relationships. I profited a great deal from my repeated analyses, the last occasion being followed by a new marriage and two children—and thus one of the most beautiful and fruitful periods of my life began.

I personally suffered a great deal, particularly in Paris, where my colleagues (with a few exceptions, like Polish-born Janine Chasseguet-Smirgel[31] and Hungarian-born Béla Grünberger), the leading intellectuals, did not want to acknowledge any of the realities and cruelties of the Bolshevik regime and the senseless deaths of many millions of people. Was this also the workings of the Irrational? Dissenting opinions at the time were punished in Paris by ignoring or casting out those who held them. In this circle, Hannah Arendt, Raymond Aron, Arthur Koestler, and Albert Camus "did not exist". The publication in French of my book on fanaticism was celebrated on the front page of *Le Monde*. Ten days later, however, through pressure from the French communist party, it was not talked about any more and even disappeared from the shops. Who was being accused of anti-fanaticism? It also caused me much pain to be seen as a die-hard reactionary, which I never was.

---

[31] In spite of her degree from the rather leftist London School of Economics.

André E. Haynal

Judit: What was the approach at the psychoanalytic institute in Geneva?

André: It was a "middle group" type of institute....

Judit: Isn't the middle group type of organization characteristic of London?

André: That was the original model. In Paris, Lacanians were one of the extremes. The others could be called Middle Groups. One of them was what's called the APF, which united prominent thinkers. That group managed to allow a lot of independent thinking. Let me only mention a few names: Laplanche,[32] Pontalis, Anzieu[33], and Granoff.[34] While they were closer to the humanities, the ones in Zurich and the Germans were closer to scientific thinking, like biology, sociology, psychology, and so on. The Parisians mainly preferred literature and philosophy in their way of conceptualizing psychoanalysis although many of them couldn't even read Freud in the original. Lengthy discussions about Freud uses of the word nachträglich and about the meaning of the noun, Nachträglicheit, expresses simply the idea that for Freud, reactions are not always immediate but arise after a latency so that nachträglich is to be understood as a time "after an event"; it is translated "officially" and awkwardly into English as "deferred action". All that, on the basis of very questionable translations of the Freudian texts by people who didn't really possess the German language. According to these authors, time, for Freud, is not a linear concept but the recurrence of certain elements of the past suddenly taking on greater significance than what they originally had. That conception can be true

---

[32] The dictionary that defines the conceptual system of psychoanalysis (*Vocabulaire de la psychanalyse*) is associated with Jean Laplanche and Jean-Bernard Lefêve-Pontalis (1967) and has been translated into virtually every major language. Laplanche (1924–2012) was a professor at the Sorbonne, and Pontalis (1924–2013) was the editor of a Sartrian cultural journal.

[33] Didier Anzieu (1923–1999) was a professor in Paris and the author of a key book on Freud's dreams (1986).

[34] The rediscovery and renaissance of Ferenczi's works in Paris is associated, in part, with Wladimir Granoff (2001).

or erroneous; what I contend is whether its basis lies in Freud's considerations. All this controversy raised by the meaning Freud could have attributed to that little word nachträglich... Talmudian or biblical exegesis?

Judit: So a child doesn't develop linearly but with leaps forward and backward.

André: Yes, that's Nachträglichkeit, the leap backward. So they think differently in Paris. I thought that I knew Freud, and it turned out that it's possible to know and interpret him differently. Later, I came to know that "British Freud," and then I realized that there's a different interpretation of him in each culture.

Judit: The text is viewed through different lenses in each culture, and the approach is through the added value that comes from your own culture.

André: That seemed very alien to me. As I came from Budapest through Vienna to Zurich, I was in an alien place but I didn't feel culturally alien. When I got to Geneva from Zurich later, I became a cultural alien again there—and particularly as a psychoanalyst. The analysts in Geneva and Paris were engaged in analysis all day, and in that constantly closed situation they developed a certain arrogance. They always thought they knew and saw things better. That somehow played a role in professional and social life as well, in the hierarchy, where you could find candidates and junior and senior members, and the seniors believed that they were far more right than the candidates, who were still only at the beginning of their careers, even if they were thirty or forty years old.

Judit: Are you saying that the Parisian SPP represented a conservative, hierarchical school model, and not a democratic educational system based on a respect for autonomy of the members in training?

André: The British or our colleagues in Zurich were more or less freer. I'd say my first psychoanalytic years in a Francophone area were spent in an atmosphere that wasn't particularly appealing.

Judit: Are we now talking about your years in Geneva?

André: Yes, in Geneva and my visits to Paris. That's when we get to the next act, when a number of things change, particularly due to the fact that members had joined different schools, engaged in new approaches to analysis, and so we saw the dissolution of the community whose authoritarian operation had sustained the previous system. It had been authority-based, so it had forced the young to make compromises. In the 10–15 years since then, the atmosphere has changed a lot, and the young are also recognized.

Judit: The multicultural influence is also present in what you're saying. It's very difficult to live in a world determined by multiculturalism because there's a great complexity in it, and our ability to tolerate complexity is always less than the complexity of the world that surrounds us. So we all inevitably filter and react to certain things: those that don't cause cognitive dissonance or threaten our integrity. Perhaps we can learn to treat different, ill-fitting factors as cultural particulars and not to exclude the parts that don't fit properly.

André: That's also seminal.

Judit: And you've run into an analyst, whose ability to tolerate complexity we both might see as reaching far beyond the norm of his age.

André: Are you talking about my first analysis?

Judit: No, about Ferenczi.[35]

André: That "encounter", let's call it "discovery" came much later.

Judit: I think there may have been a number of reasons for your encountering Ferenczi in the end. There may be a factor from culture or from the history of identity. After all, he was a Budapest analyst. Your dealing with Ferenczi meant getting to know the life's work of a person who was able to bear the complicated nature of complexity

---

[35] In my eyes, the most important of Freud's follower, for a long time excluded from the memory of psychoanalysts (see later).

in an exceptionally intelligent way—the fact that things are sometimes ill-fitting. Emotionally, of course, he wasn't as free as he was intellectually. But in his thinking he had a basic need not to short-circuit the problematic questions. Short-circuited things hinder the freedom to think. I sense a parallel between you and Ferenczi in this context. But let's return to Geneva, where you were given an important role.

André: I had a role in the opening-up when our generation took over the leadership.

Judit: When did that happen?

André: In 1976–77.

Judit: As far as I know, you were the president of the Swiss Psychoanalytic Society between 1976 and 1979.

André: There was an opening. When I was elected to the leadership along with my colleagues, although it wasn't a revolutionary act in and of itself, it was still considered a great change. Bertrand Cramer, who was around the same age as me, became the secretary, and a Kleinian colleague Marcelle Spira, the head of the training committee. Until then, she had never been recognized as a "real analyst"—.

Judit: Did you also work with her as an analyst?

André: I was later in supervision with Spira, but then she became, as I just mentioned, the chair of the training committee, so the key positions were all given to people who had played no major role up to then. Given all this, I would say that it was a new beginning, which—even with its bumps—brought about a noticeably freer atmosphere and way of thinking. Many analysts had not been satisfied with our training and had gone to Paris or London for further experience. It was also important that a great deal of interplay had developed within the society itself.

Judit: Talk a bit about that structure. There was the institute in Geneva, the psychoanalytic institute in Zurich, and there was Basel, Bern, and Lugano. There were therefore five local institutions tied *to five different cities, and five—more or less different—sorts of atmosphere and institutional structure. So, is it right to regard the Swiss Psychoanalytic Society as a united form of representation of different institutions operating in five cities?*

André: The Swiss Society also meets regularly. Everyone is a member of the Society, whether that person is from Geneva or Zurich or elsewhere. Once every other month, on Saturdays, they get together for a meeting from morning to evening in Bern, halfway between the main cities.

Judit: So besides the local level of operation, there's a federal level. But you wanted to add something to Geneva.

André: Initially—compared to Zurich—I felt an antipathy for the functioning of the group in Geneva. Then later, with the changes, the atmosphere was renewed and became freer. There were also a number of interesting young people attending my seminars, and working with them always turned out to be very exciting.

Psychoanalysis and the University

In this situation, it became possible for me to practice psychoanalysis and teach psychotherapy. For the latter, it meant that it was now possible to raise my interest in academia, by devoting time to it, and to conceive of my own new ideas. The years I spent in Geneva were characterized by balanced stability. In my practice, I primarily conducted analyses; at the university, I held theoretical classes and clinical presentations about the psychological problems in medicine; at the psychiatric institutions, on the technique of psychotherapy; and at the psychoanalytic institute, on psychoanalysis.

To Judit: *In this environment, I was part of the University Department of Psychiatry, where my main task was teaching psychotherapy and treating somatically ill patients in the general hospital—including what was called "psychosomatic illnesses," in the large sense of this term. I worked with a group of very interested* collaborators, of which the most important were Pr. Willy Pasini, who was in contact and collaborated with the department of gynecology, and Dr. Marc Archinard, for the rest of the hospital patients. I wrote a book with them (Haynal, Pasini, 1978) about this kind of medicine, which became an important teaching material in French-speaking and some other countries. These activities complemented each other very well with my psychoanalytic basic orientation, practice, and research. Some of my books and papers about psychoanalysis bear witness to this.

I had time to think, read, and write; it was a gift from the gods. This wonderful situation came slowly to an end through the bureaucratization and the subjugation of the psycho-professions by the state and insurance companies.

In this book I originally intended to give an account of my experiences, impressions and ideas centered around psychoanalysis. There is, however, another side to my professional life, which although no less inspired by psychoanalysis, really touches *psychiatry* in its proper sense. Such a double activity was historically part of our traditions, as Freud, Ferenczi, Balint, Winnicott and many others were interested in both fields. Teaching psychiatric interview techniques, psychotherapeutic procedures, encounters with general practitioners in what were called "Balint groups" (listening to other practitioners recount their encounters with their patients) took only a little part of my time.

In psychiatry, daily encounters with deeply disturbed patients, and the caretakers intensely preoccupied with these people, implied the sacrifice of years of existence on the edge of what I could offer as an answer. My conviction that opening up the classical medically modeled psychiatry was an important step in the evolution of this discipline and practice at that time. Psychoanalysis sensitized us, as psychiatrists, to *listen* to the patient, who, until then, was simply considered as "talking crazy" and not as expressing himself/herself in another difficult language. Instead of excluding them from everyday life and keeping them in sanatoriums and asylums, we offered them collaboration in working on their life plan within their normal environment in the city. In other words, instead of treating them as medical objects, we lived close to them as similar human beings. I am happy to have been part of this great endeavor in Geneva, which transformed psychiatric healing and support activities and replaced the old obsolete anatomic vision of mental diseases, which brought nothing significant to ameliorate the care for this population, with an approach to mental illness that offered support, inclusion, participation rather than exclusion, removal, separation. How much did I learn from group meetings with these patients, their discourse, their confessions displaying intimacy and revealing new fundamental insights! In fact, during that time, I had two jobs—equally two passions. I loved both and one relieved me from the other. I was part of a great movement of a humanization of psychiatry, stimulated by the evolution of human sciences.

I met the transformational force of psychoanalysis in the psychiatric field and in supervising medical practitioners, nurses and social workers. My involvement in the *medical field* was especially challenging for me, as I was proceeding in a virgin field at the intersection of medicine and psychiatry—in the continuation of Balint's previous efforts—where awareness of the presence of psychological factors in illness and in caring relationships was until then sinfully absent.

These experiences convinced me that psychoanalytic thinking, with its particular insights, can be of great help in social life. I will speak more about this in the chapter about fanaticism—the great evil of 20th and 21st centuries, and the efforts made to cure us of it.

At the time, the contributions of psychoanalysis were at the forefront of interest at the institution. Nowadays, however, the time seems to be ripe to examine how complementary gains in knowledge made by different research, for example neuroscience, might complete or shed further light on this field. Even in admitting that they play only a modest role in the bedside activities, progress is made. The role of the contributions of other methods, for example cognitive-behavioral, also search for their place to be included in a non-sectarian cognitive science that would establish a discipline of studying the *Mind and Brain as an organ of transformation.*

Encounters with the Irrational: My Story

Technique and Method: The Psychoanalytical Practice

The only source of knowledge is experience.
ALBERT EINSTEIN

Judit: I remember you once made subtle distinctions between technique and method. Where do you see the difference now between those two as an analyst?

André: I think technique actually suggests that there is a prescribed way of operating, as with machines which you can only operate if you follow the instructions. If there is a technique, there are instructions—operating principles—to accompany it. As if it had proceeded from the very nature of things. Simplifying it slightly, it also calls to mind this technical world of ours. Freud could certainly not have anticipated it. Today, in our understanding, technique means something different than at Freud's time. As far as method (methodos) is concerned, it is the hodos (a path); a meta (through something); that is, a large road, a more general attitude, or a direction to be taken. This notion forms a part of philosophical traditions that later also entered the sciences. We encounter the concept of "method" as early as Aristotle's work, and so there is a long philosophical tradition behind the notion of taking a particular path. That's not technique! In psychoanalysis, I think it's rather that Freud dreamed of a situation (what a psychoanalytic session would be like) and, on the basis of these dreams, a long historical evolution formed what it has slowly become. There are no precise or minute rules as are involved in 'technique'.

Judit: This distinction between technique and method somehow fits well into your life story. After all, you also had an education in philosophy and not only in medicine.

André: Actually, I loved the history of philosophy. It inspired me, although I was not consciously thinking about it at the time ... that, one day, as I attempted to shed light on a few chapters in the history of psychoanalytic thinking, I'd be influenced by its model.

Judit: Somehow, your sensitivity to philosophy and your attraction to history and medicine motivated you all at once.

André: Medicine has influenced me to the extent that, since Freud, we all believe that what he created is also at once a method of healing—which, of course, yet again, is debatable. Because healing means that there is a disorder, perhaps an illness, and a drive, a desire, or a definite will for a person to get out of it, while we provide aid that surely leads them to that goal. However that seems not true for everybody in the case of psychoanalysis.

Judit: After your book on fanaticism, you published your studies on techniques in analysis.

André: Besides books on depression, fanaticism, and orphans, there are two other volumes, one on psychoanalytic technique (with emphasis on Ferenczi and Balint) and one booklet on Ferenczi.

Judit: Technique appears in your book such that it is already tied to particular names and ways of thinking, which can be clearly separated from other types of thinking. Did you originally write your book Controversies in Psychoanalytic Method (1989) in French?

André: Yes, I wrote those books in French, in the middle of a debate where the French psychoanalyst Lacan challenged the "classical" technique with unusual time schedules (for example, short sessions, etc.), which brought about a passionate controversy. That was the first volume on that topic area, followed by the publication of the correspondence between Freud and Ferenczi (Brabant, Falzeder, Giampieri-Deutsch, 1993; Falzeder, Brabant 1996, 2000)...

Judit: We've returned to Ferenczi yet again... How would you approach psychoanalysis today?

André: It begins by my attempting to say how the psychoanalytic process comes about. I think you can conceive it in three parts, three acts. The first is the act of luring, mutual seduction. That is, the patients are invited to come to my warm room three or four times a week, lie on a couch, possibly relaxing, and then say anything they *want to, anything that comes to mind, without end. Then we come to their traumas, their traumatization. In my understanding, everyone has basic trauma(s) in their life. The third part of the analysis is to understand and process these. As for what role various influences and emotions play in this and how we arrive at putting our understandings into words, that's what I attempt to work out in my books afterwards using a few historical examples.*

Judit: So you're also saying that the non-verbal communication that occurs during analysis involves everything, right? From the way they sit to the silence and breathing to intonation, to understanding...?

André: ...the understanding of the analyst to begin with.

Judit: The communication on the part of both participants is significant. Do you think that we devote more attention to that today?

André: More attention than Freud did, yes. It plays a very important role for Ferenczi and none at all for Hartmann or Lacan. Lacan said that analysis is (only) text. Lacan exclusively limited his and his students' attention to text. I think the English school has played a major role in maintaining a much broader clinical tradition and paying a great deal of attention to non-verbal communication also.

Judit: How is it in Switzerland?

André: The truth is that every Swiss institute is a unique, eclectic mix of various influences. The situation in Geneva is different from that in Zurich and Basel. Geneva represents a broad coalition just like London. The French classics, the French mildly Lacanians and semi-Lacanians, the British Kleinians, the South American Kleinians, and representatives of what is referred to as the English independent group are all present in Geneva through their influence. There is no "Swiss school," as such. Everyone is different in some area—they couldn't or didn't want to establish a school. When I was young, culturally, psychoanalytic Switzerland was as much French in its attitude as it was English or American. It might seem like a paradox, but if you think about it, all of those whom we call now English or American are primarily immigrants from German-speaking territories. They returned later, after the war, for lectures and conferences to Europe, like—for example, to Zurich.

Judit: Whom do you have in mind?

André: I remember Richard Sterba,[36] but there were others as well: Paula Heimann[37] and Erich Fromm.[38]

Judit: Where do you feel most at home? In which psychoanalytic group?

André: Mainly as an independent: I take my own eclectic path. If, as a person, I were to commit myself in a group I couldn't fully identify with any of them, but if I had to—then I'd most likely go with one of the British groups, for example with Winnicott and Bion, as well as with Balint and those we call the independents. Unlike some of my colleagues in Geneva, I'm not a Kleinian, although I used to be under moderate Kleinian influence and continue to be today.

Judit: What is Kleinian about your way of thinking?

André: I think that it was the Kleinians that preserved and stressed the importance of clinical psychoanalysis after World War II and during the years of mourning after Freud's death. Others established a number of theories, mostly tightly empiricist, through which a few things became increasingly dry and uninteresting, for example, in ego psychology. My attachment to the problems of clinical psychoanalysis may have something characteristically similar to the Kleinian endeavor.

---

[36] Richard Sterba (1898–1989), a psychoanalyst from Vienna, immigrated to the United States out of solidarity with his colleagues, who were forced to flee Nazism.
[37] Paula Heimann (1899–1982), a German psychoanalyst who immigrated to London, was a student of Melanie Klein's but later became independent of the Kleinian group.
[38] Erich Fromm (1900–1980) was an independent (south-) German psychoanalyst, who later lived and worked in the U.S. and Mexico and spent his last days in Italian-speaking Switzerland.

Encounters with the Irrational: My Story

To Ernst: In London people were preoccupied with clinical psychoanalysis, based on the problems that surfaced in the relationship. In nuce, this had also been the case in Zurich. There we also talked about relationship problems, perhaps not so much as in London, but in England there was a completely different atmosphere, also among the Kleinians. Whatever one may say or criticize about "Kleinian" problems, those analysts really always proceeded from a real relationship experience in an analysis, and not from a construction. I think that many people have a wrong idea about this today, particularly those who do not like the Kleinians. They think that the latter force preconceived images upon a case in an ideological way, so to speak, whereas in my opinion quite the contrary happened at the time; maybe not necessarily by Klein herself, but by analysts such as Paula Heimann, Herbert Rosenfeld, Michael Balint, and others I got to know in London. Everything was based on what happened between analyst and analysand. Rosenfeld for instance was in my experience one of the greatest persons working analytically. I remember that he presented a case and then said, it was sometime early in the year, maybe March or April: "Well, I thought this year I can't interrupt this treatment, so I won't go on summer vacation". This was completely different from the rational and ideological approach in average Parisian psychoanalysis.

To Judit: *It is that clinical interest and the theories closely tied to it that led me to be the first one—and the only one for a long time—among those who were referred to as "the young" in my generation whom our President Raymond de Saussure[39] trusted to hold a seminar.*

Judit: When did that happen? In the mid-seventies?

André: Rather at the end of those years. He wanted me to discuss Freud in the seminar. Or, more precisely, he really wanted me not to deal exclusively with the post-Freudians. Raymond de Saussure played the role of a well-intentioned father in my life. He had returned from America in the Sixties, but that's another story. He was

---

[39] Raymond de Saussure (1894–1971). See later text.

a Swiss patrician; we might say an "aristocrat"—although there is no real aristocracy in Switzerland. The city's bourgeoisie didn't like him much because he ignored local Calvinist morality by marrying four times.

After World War II, he came back to his hometown. He became the central, fatherly figure of the Geneva group. He was the first to tell me, "After what you've lived through, you should be dealing with the history of psychoanalysis." Interestingly, that statement was prompted by his intuition. He had no rational reason for it. He himself wrote a book about the forerunners of psychoanalysis (Chertok, de Saussure, 1973) and I also learned hypnosis in part from him. He offered hypnosis courses at the Universities of Geneva and Lausanne. He was known to be a special, unusual personality.

Judit: In what respect?

André: In every respect: he was a nonconformist. What's more, he was a nonconformist in an era in which such an attitude was not easily accepted in orthodox psychoanalytical circles. Even so, he was considered a respected member of the Freudian establishment, and he had free access to Anna Freud. But, despite all that, he did whatever he wanted. He wrote his book on the forerunners of Freud in a spirit that suggested that Freud was actually not as original as had been claimed. I remember a supervision in his library in a mansion in the middle of the city of Geneva. He had a wonderful library with masses of books from the nineteenth century, which he bought in Paris. He told me by way of explanation, "Haynal, we psychoanalysts are too sensitive." He very much stood out from his surroundings. He also had money. He traveled throughout Europe in the twenties and thirties. He had a carefree life, allowing himself to be himself, even at the cost of strange and extreme choices.

Judit: This very influential, original man encouraged you to...
André: ...as I said, he permitted history to form a greater part of my interests, for one thing, and he entrusted me with an important seminar, at such a 'young age'. He was starting to grow old, and

that's when he left to me all the topics he had been dealing with. There were good and bad sides to all that. It was through his influence that I reached the point where I read Balint in Paris and discovered the first generation, including Ferenczi as well. Ferenczi's work was starting to be published in French at the time, translated by Judith Dupont and her group, and that was when I announced my first Ferenczi seminar in Geneva; it was my 'first contact' with Ferenczi.

Judit: *And what did you read? The three volumes, his collected works (Ferenczi, 1980)?*

André: *I think I studied the four-volume publication (in French), yes. That was at about the same time that I started going to London. Partly also to improve my English. It had a great impact on me that I was able to participate in the supervisions there.*

A SOJOURN IN NORTH AMERICA, AT LAST

It was roughly at this time that I met Michael Balint in London a few times. He encouraged me to study earlier issues of psychoanalytic journals instead of second-rate articles by contemporary authors. If I remember well, for example, he recommended to me the topic of narcissism from the 1910s. He was one of two, the other being Raymond de Saussure, who encouraged me to deal with the history of psychoanalysis.

Judit: *Did you discuss cases?*

André: *Yes, that was important for me. Just as when I met Michael Balint. He was very benevolent with me.*

To Ernst: *It began when he, who was the president of the British society at the time, organized a kind of conferences for English-speaking members of the European societies. This was an offer to train in the "English way", particularly in the way of the English Independent group. The whole course consisted of case presentations and discussions, it was very praxis-oriented, and very*

André E. Haynal

Figure 24: Michael Balint

different from how it was done in Paris. This was very much to my liking, after similar courses in Paris in February. The institute of the SPP offered these training courses to people from the French provinces, but in the eyes of many Parisians Geneva is anyhow a province of France… So we too got invited; one inscribed, one paid, one could have one's cases supervised, and it was a good way to get to know the French way. But to return to Balint: He held these seminars every second summer, for about a week or a bit less, maybe four days, with distinguished supervisors like Winnicott. Other very good people participated, though not Klein herself, but for example Herbert Rosenfeld. I always went to Rosenfeld; I always went to Winnicott; and it was really the "fine art" of psychoanalysis. It was very practical and very English. Afterwards I had personal contact with Balint and told him that I would like to come to him for a few supervisions from Geneva, on Fridays or so, and he accepted. So I went to him for a few times. Then I decided that I would have to perfect my English. My English was mediocre, not satisfactory, so I enrolled in three or four consecutive summer courses, for a month each. The courses were in the mornings, from 8 to 12 or 1 or 2, using the modern methods of the time, like listening to yourself via microphone and headphones, one's accent was corrected, etc. I liked this method very much, and we also read good texts by Priestley, Maugham, etc. In the afternoons I went to Peter Hildebrand at the Tavistock Clinic. He had been a Jewish refugee child in Switzerland during the war, and then had studied in French at the Sorbonne for some time. He was very open-minded, and he also liked French Switzerland. He introduced me to the Tavistock Clinic, where, in the afternoons, I could participate in the consultations, for example with Bowlby. It was really very interesting. This was how I learned my English.

Judit: Did you speak to Balint in English?

André: Always in English only. He had a terrible accent. On top of that, my patient, whom I discussed with him, spoke French, so all this complicated my situation quite a bit. Remember that in those days I didn't speak Hungarian with anyone.

Judit: It's interesting that you and Balint avoided Hungarian. It seems to me it would have been natural for you to speak to each other in your mother tongue....

André: I think he didn't want to. There was this sort of émigré mentality. Among those who had emigrated in the 1930s or at the end of that decade, some never, ever returned to Hungary and didn't speak the language any longer. Balint himself only went back twice. We felt we had resettled and would live and die in our new countries. It didn't even occur to me that I'd be able to return to Hungary soon. I didn't even go there for 25 years, before the late 1970s. It was a major separation, a major break.

The period in Geneva also made it possible to participate, twice, in a visiting professorship, a year each time at Stanford University in Northern California. I represented a psychoanalytic orientation in interaction with outstanding cognitivists and neuroscientific scholars. I learned a lot from them. Some of them became friends for life like Barr and Suesan Taylor, Mary-Ann and Paul Ekman, Annelies Korner and Kal Kalman, Alexandra and Wolfgang Lederer, as well as the psychoanalysts Mardi Horowitz and Alvin Rosenfeld. With others I had a more distant relationship: Tom Gonda, Stewart Agras, David Spiegel. A unique place for the world's best universities, under palm trees and sunshine. I had time left to write, and I was given the opportunity to contribute to teaching residents. What a treat to profit from all the advantages of some great research universities in the U.S., especially in the excessively stimulating human environment of California.

In the same period, I was also a candidate for a scholarship from the Kennedy Foundation to carry out studies in medical ethics, which was then a relatively new perspective. However, I gave it up and remained faithful to psychoanalysis.

During my stay at Stanford, I was able to improve my English so that it became a real working language, and I profited more than before from English-language literature.

Moreover, I had the opportunity to take up a new analysis.

Judit: With whom?

André: Emanuel Windholz[40] was recommended to me by Pető.[41] I kept in touch with Pető in New York. He had some idea that Windholz was possibly of Hungarian descent, from Slovakia, and

---

[40] Emanuel Windholz (1903–1986), a European and American psychoanalyst, was born in the Hungarian town of Hronec (in present-day Slovakia). He studied in Brno, Prague, and Paris. He then did his residency in Košice/Kassa, Prague, and Berlin. He went to Moshe Wulff in Berlin and Francis Déry in Prague for analysis. Between 1936 and 1939, after a number of members of the group had emigrated, he became the head of the Psychoanalytic Study Group in Prague, but after the German occupation of Czechoslovakia, he also escaped to the United States. There, he participated in the establishment of the San Francisco Psychoanalytic Society, in which he held a number of key offices – as he did later in the American Psychoanalytic Association.

[41] Endre (Andrew) Pető left Hungary with his family in 1949. First, they immigrated to Australia, and then, in 1956, they resettled in New York City. He became a member of the New York Psychoanalytic Society and a training analyst there and, later, its president.

that he had studied in Prague. Actually, he was born in Hungary (in what's now Slovakia), studied medicine in Prague and psychoanalysis in Berlin, and immigrated to America in 1939—strangely, we thought he spoke Hungarian at first. At least, Pető thought so, but it turned out that wasn't true at all. We started communicating in German, but then I realized he didn't speak anymore German either. So, in the end, we did the sessions in American English. It went very well. It was a very important period and an intensive year, my so-called sabbatical year.

Judit: Of your three periods of analysis, you said the one in California occupied a central place.

André: Emanuel Windholz, who was well known in San Francisco, was an interesting man. He was also inspired by Ferenczi's ideas, although I never talked to him about that, for example, about technique. Later, I met him at the conference in Hamburg,[42] but we barely managed to greet each other because I had to leave the following day: that's when my daughter was born in California. I was never able to talk to Windholz again after that. He passed away a year later. Long after my analysis, I had the feeling that he had a variety of technical interventions, for instance, the techniques of forced recollection. You know how it is: you remember a few scenes from the sessions. I remember one of those scenes not because it was especially important, but because it took me by surprise. At the end of our analysis, he claimed that I'd said that he was no longer there, that is, that he was dead to me, or something like that. So he insisted that we try to imagine that he's died, and, although I tried in vain to prove that I hadn't meant it that way and that I hadn't intended to hurt him, he insisted. "Now you imagine that you're reading on the second page of The San Francisco Chronicle that Emanuel Windholz has just died and...." He had a sort of powerful, somewhat persistent method, which I hadn't experienced with other classical analysts.

---

[42] The 34th Congress of the International Psychoanalytical Association, Hamburg, 1985, the first one in Germany since the Second World War.

André E. Haynal

BACK IN GENEVA, A NEW LIFE

> *The good life is one inspired by love and guided by knowledge.*
> BERTRAND RUSSELL

After returning to Geneva, my second wife and I finalized our divorce, and I remained by myself for three years.

Then I met Véronique who was finishing her MA training at an American university.

Judit: What was her topic?

André: The relationship between nonverbal communication and emotional life. We moved in together in 1984.... Then, in '85, Cleo was born, very soon after. From the outset, a relationship developed between us that was harmonious, one that lacked any rationalization or hesitation. Véronique's father was a general practitioner outside Geneva. They lived in an outskirt called Chêne-Bourg, three kilometers from the place we live in now. When Véronique was 18 or 19 years old, she worked in Germany with epileptic patients, later she left to study in the U.S. for a year, then she went to Zurich and studied at the ETH (Technical University) Zurich. Back in Geneva, she studied psychology and worked with psychotic and neurotic children, and, afterwards, she dealt with sexology. So it's true that she's from Geneva, but she's lived in the U.S., she's lived in Zurich, so she's not someone who's bound to one place. Her first relatively long, five-year job was in sexology in Geneva, so she worked at a nonconformist institution. The topic of sexology isn't exactly held in high regard among the old Geneva families.

Judit: It's interesting that your third wife has roots in Geneva but has also had a cosmopolitan experience.

André: It's extremely interesting because she's from an old Calvinist family that came over to Geneva from France even before the persecution in the 1500s. The family became citizens of Geneva 500 years ago, and they celebrated that recently.

Judit: They were Calvinists, like your mother's family.

André: Yes, the majority of her family settled in Geneva, but a part of the family moved to Zurich.

Judit: So besides the cosmopolitanism, the family also experienced some persecution.

André: Yes. From a modern-day perspective, she's from a traditional family, which is still not traditional in the sense that Véronique's aunt, that is, her mother's older sister, married a man in Rome and then lived in Naples with her husband. Her mother's other sibling worked in the U.S. as a book merchant, and the third one lived in northern Italy with a Genevian-Italian spouse. Véronique and her siblings regularly spent time in their summers with the aunt who lived in Naples. For Véronique, Italian is a childhood language, the way German is for me.

SLOWLY BUT SURELY, THE FAMILY BECAME COSMOPOLITAN: KIDS

Judit: You're truly mobile despite your strict value system. We might even say that mobility has characterized the life of the Haynal family. It's a family tradition, if you will. At the same time, you're also rebellious, if I may say so.

André: You may.

Judit: In your third marriage, we've found certain very subtle shared areas of experience that linked your wife's life's path to your own. In fact, the paths and fortunes of the two families have much in common. I suspect that your coming to know each other was an experience of discovery. And your own first child was born.

André: That was a miracle! It's completely different for a man than for a woman....

The man sees the changes during the whole time on the shape, on the silhouette, of the woman and other things, too, for example, the

Figure 25: Daughter Cleo born June 1985

heartbeat, but still. When I was on duty every other day in the hospital in Bülach, I witnessed a large number of births. So birth wasn't a new experience for me—still, that birth was like a miracle: suddenly there was Cleo! I'll never forget the way she arrived. In California, where she was born, they lay the child on the mother's body.... They gave the baby to Véronique right away. And they didn't put any drops in her eyes, nothing, and they were able to come home the second or third day.... It was human, state-of-the-art, a minima medical treatment.

Judit: You once said that your daughter looked around....

André: She did, and it was incredible: she arrived, and she looked at the operating stand, and she looked at her mother, of course, and she also looked at the doctor.... When I assisted with births as a young physician in Bülach, it was completely different. The nurses took the child away, gave it a bath, and prevented it from seeing normally because of the eye drops, and I don't remember anymore what else they did. In California, there was no such ritual; the baby was handed to the mother, and the two of them cuddled—there was something infinitely moving and captivating about it. I think the truth still is—and there are surely many who don't like to hear this—the greatest joys in life are tied to biology, to the body, i.e., to love and sexuality, and to our relationships with children. They're tied to instincts, mostly to the instinct of survival of the species. And a child is certainly tied to man's personal survival. Perhaps that's the deeper meaning of the Freudian significance of sexuality and its links to the ego.

Judit: I rarely see you moved, but when we talk about Cleo you're very often moved.

André: Because she was the first one. It's completely unfair when everyone acts as though there's equality....

Judit: That's actually a mental effort, a compass, but in reality and especially in matters of emotion it doesn't really exist.

André: The great unfairness is that, although I've always loved my daughter, I was unable to spare her from living through difficulties in her teenage years, like those I'd had. Cleo was the first. When David was young, he often asked, would Cleo always be older than he was? David always had memorable things to say. He was very

Figure 26: Son David born March 1987

young—he must have been three years old—when he stated that the mirror was no good. When asked why not, he responded that he was much nicer-looking than what he saw in the mirror.

Judit: Your second child came along quickly.

André: One and a half years later. That's how we wanted it. We wanted to avoid a long reign for the only child. Both Véronique and I.

Judit: So with the birth of Cleo and David, you again obtained something that you had not known before. What kind of father would you have liked to be? What kind of father are you?

André: I was very close to the children. I played with them a lot, as much as my profession and my situation allowed. I say it like that because after each vacation it was very difficult to leave in the morning and only return in the evening. I think I suffered more from that than the kids did, from that industrial way of life, the hospital lifestyle of doctors. I was not with them as much during the day as I would have liked. For example, when I went to a congress, which was very important—wherever it was, France, Israel, the U.S., Germany—we always took the children with us, if possible. And they proudly declared that they had traveled and seen the whole world. I didn't want us to be without them even for five days, so we took them with us everywhere.

Judit: So your children grew into an international, cosmopolitan lifestyle, but not under the obligation of immigration....

André: I didn't want them to have the immigrant experience. They didn't learn Hungarian at first because I didn't want them to carry the burden of immigration. They were born in the U.S. They're American, and, through their mother, they're also Genevian Swiss. Later, following the regime change, we came to Hungary more often. Before that, we didn't come much, only for my parents' funerals. Cleo wanted to learn Hungarian, and she can speak my native language a little bit. It was her initiative. No one forced her.

Judit: Tell me, the fact that both children were born in the U.S. and that they're also U.S. citizens by birth, which is a great privilege, was that your conscious decision?

André: It just happened. It wasn't something we'd engineered, but since we were there.... See, after my years as a visiting professor, I maintained contacts at Stanford, and we had a lot of mutual projects. It would have been senseless to return to Geneva for the child to be born there. And we also thought that Cleo would have the opportunity as an American citizen to be even freer than we were. And then we said, what's good for one of them, Cleo, David should get, too.

Judit: If David couldn't be the first, he should have no disadvantage in terms of where he was born....

André: As you can see, we tried to treat both of them the same and not to give advantages to one over the other (and thus give causes for jealousy). I was very careful about two or three things. One was not to have a spirit of authority within the family because both Véronique and I had suffered a lot from that. I acted like that because as a child I had to do what my father wanted—if it didn't happen, then he got very upset and started shouting. My mother also did more or less what my father wanted, and then they left each other anyway for a while....

An important part of bringing up our children was allowing them freedom. Another consideration was to have their intellect develop. Often, I'd ask them fun quiz questions during dinner to stimulate their desire for knowledge.... It actually just happened, but it seemed to be a lot of fun for them, too.

Judit: Tell me one of them.

André: It also depended on where we were. For example, having visited a country, I would ask, do you remember what the capital is? I asked age-appropriate questions. They really loved it. For example, when the Soviet Union collapsed, I asked them which country Baku is in. There was a huge world map in the breakfast nook in our kitchen, and they ran to the map to find Baku. Yes, the world map was always in front of them as well as the map of Switzerland.... It's very difficult to describe it well—life consists of such tiny things. For a very long time, until David was about ten years old, we went swimming together almost every day after I came home in the evening.

Judit: So you had your male bonding?

André: Yes, we did. Cleo didn't like the water because it was too cold for her. She pretended to be the refined young lady. In other situations, like her passion for horseback riding, it was very different.

Every Sunday when we were at home, we went biking with the kids or skiing in the winter.

Judit: Would you say something more about parenting principles?

André: What kind of parents would we have liked to be? Inspiring and liberal. Véronique was very supportive of that in me. We agreed entirely because she'd come from a relatively quiet, middle-class family, where it was her mother who imposed discipline ... in a cold, Calvinist manner, while her warmer father was socialized, rather typically, in the physician's worldview of the 1920s and '30s.

Judit: What did that physician's worldview mean? What made it typical?

André: One example: When my mother underwent surgery for breast cancer, my father associated her depressive mood with hormonal changes—and not with her suffering.... Although he also went to a "Balint group", Véronique's father would have thought similarly.

Judit: ...in terms of biological explanations.

André: We tried to form a free, liberal-minded, and understanding family.

Judit: I think if you have a well-integrated personality, you work the same way on managing a family in practice as you do in principle. In your way of thinking about the world or in your cooperation with your children, you follow certain principles consistently, even if not always consciously.

André: Let me remind you of something you said once: One possible measure of an analyst is whether you can bring your children up harmoniously. Sometimes other influences prevail, however. So there are constitutionally (even if we don't know what that is) more difficult children, or those who are frequently ill and thus become problematic. I think what we can all gain from our analyses is that we become better (not perfect) parents, not passing on bad examples and types of relationships.

Judit: You know, that's very important. That's the fundamental value of analysis. Once, one of my patients told me that the greatest benefit she reaped from therapy was that she became a far better mother to her third, "reparation" child, as she referred to him, than she had been to her two teenagers earlier. She could not have been without the therapy experience and her new knowledge of her own self. Another patient of mine, a man, also added that one of the results that pointed to the future of his efforts in therapy was that through it a neurotic repetition that had lasted for a number of generations would stop. That was very true, and it's good that you can conduct your life with a higher level of freedom. Psychoanalysis is a process of liberation.

André: I completely agree.

Judit: Tell me, with regard to your children and a little bit with regard to your liberal and cosmopolitan life as well … it's somehow an extension of that that Cleo now lives in the U.S., isn't it?

André: I'm sure that our influence has also played a role, and we hope it's good for her, although she lives far away from us. And she's certainly been in a good university training program.

Judit: Yes, and she's chosen that for herself. And you both approved her decision. But she didn't have to leave you behind, only grow up at a greater distance, that is, on another continent.

André: David's also succeeded in finding a place for himself, a place where he can operate best and be happiest. Both children received this as their inheritance. Sometimes, of course, I ask myself—just as anyone else would ask—whether I have cause for a bit of a bad conscience because I thought that it would be better for Cleo to live in California rather than in tiny Geneva. And is that even true? After all, she's experienced a lot of difficulties there that I'm not going to discuss now. So that will remain a question for some time.

DISCOVERING A SERENE PSYCHOANALYST: FERENCZI IN CORRESPONDENCE WITH FREUD

To Judit: *André: Balint drew my attention to Ferenczi and the Parisians, such as Wladimir Granoff.*[43] *I've always said that I liked Balint's ideas very much, and Balint refers a lot to Ferenczi. I had a personal relationship with him. If this is my imaginary family tree, so to say, then Balint is one of my ancestors. An important movement evolved in Paris, in which Ferenczi was discovered—by Wladimir Granoff, a somewhat Lacanian analyst, along with a few others. Some analysts learned a lot from Ferenczi. Granoff belonged to the APF,*[44] *and not the SPP.*[45] *In the APF, which was an elite group, similar to the Independents in London, there were a lot of intellectually interesting people, as I have already mentioned. Why am I saying that? During my training, I didn't like to study Karl Abraham. I thought he was dry and theoretical. On the contrary, nobody ever spoke about Ferenczi in a seminar. When I became a*

---

[43] Wladimir Granoff (1924–2000), a French psychoanalyst who came from a Russian émigré family. In 1953, he was one of the rebellious young people at the psychoanalytic institute in Paris. After his break from Lacan in 1963, he retired from the psychoanalytic societies. In 1958, he was among the first in France to study Ferenczi's work.

[44] APF (Association Psychanalytique de France), one of the French psychoanalytic societies, part of the IPA.

[45] SPP (Société Psychanalytique de Paris), the Parisian psychoanalytic society, representing the French mainstream or classical trend. Among its members are André Green, Serge Lebovici, and Joyce McDougall.

training analyst, I decided to get to the bottom of the why of this question as well as to what I'd seen in Paris and heard from Balint.

Judit: When you became a training analyst, it represented a new phase.

André: They gave me seminars, and they told me that I had to cover Freud first. That was in the early 1970s. When I later became president of the Swiss Society of Psychoanalysis, I did more or less what I wanted to. I wanted to start seminars that interested me first and foremost. I wanted to know who this Ferenczi really was. I announced a seminar on Ferenczi for the students. Balint—who could be aggressive sometimes—once asked me something like, instead of reading "who knows whom", why didn't I read the old classics? I asked him, who? "Well, Ferenczi," was his response. I think it was the Parisian influence that led me to announce my seminar. We were reading Ferenczi for three years, each week.

My final intensive work was suggested by Michael's widow, Enid Balint-Edmonds. In the 1980s, she called me at Stanford to ask whether I would undertake the job of coordinating and editing, with collaborators, the publication of the Freud-Ferenczi correspondence. It was unbelievably exciting to find the manuscript—in a briefcase four floors below ground level at a bank in a London suburb. This is when Ilse Grubrich-Simitis laid her hands on the hitherto unknown manuscript of Freud's famous twelfth psychological study, which she eventually published with the title *Übersicht der Übertragungsneurosen* (Overview of the Transference Neuroses, Grubrich-Simitis, 1987). Many of the publications around Ferenczi, including his correspondence with Freud became a complicated process with debates over permissions and copyright, which I partly outlined in the introduction to the first volume of the published correspondence (Haynal, 1993). What I would like to mention here is that work with Ernst Falzeder and Éva Brabant-Gerő, and the generous assistance of Judith Dupont, opened up a new world for me. To see close up the way a genius and a very talented man thinks about psychoanalysis is magic. Seeing Freud as a man opened up new dimensions as well. I find it extremely interesting to research the background of the conception of certain of their works.

After one of my lectures, I received a comment that, in my presentation, I was much rather dealing with Freud than with Ferenczi, and that was right. What I understood about Ferenczi and his very innovative thinking with regard to technique, I published in two books (Haynal, 1988, 2002) and a few articles, some of them written with Ernst Falzeder. This correspondence, however—more precisely, certain psychoanalytic trains of thought, concepts, insights, and adaptations presented therein by both authors—provided me with new perspectives, in fact, it changed my life. The same way I think no one can become a competent biologist without spending a couple of years in a laboratory to understand the strengths and weaknesses of the procedures, I also believe that psychoanalysis itself cannot be properly understood without studying the personal background of the pioneers in the field, for example, through their correspondences. Reading Ferenczi's ideas, I gained an insight into the technical development of psychoanalysis that I demonstrated at a conference in New York and then in an article written for a volume by Lewis Aron and Adrienne Harris (Haynal, 1993).

Michael Balint, the most lively and enthusiastic friend of Ferenczi's work, left important papers behind as well. Enid Balint chose to entrust me with those documents and objects, which were brought to Geneva under my custody in 1981. Was it a symbolic gesture by Enid, the meaning of which was never spelled out? Was it, in recognition of the relationship and of the work for the publication of the Correspondence, a bit of gratitude and help? Was it simply out of trust in my capability to look after this precious material adequately, keeping it in an academic environment and out of family feuds or, worse, feuds of psychoanalytic families?...

These documents are now back in London, delivered in 2014 as I donated them to the Archives of the British Psychoanalytical Society.[46]

As for the original Freud and Ferenczi manuscript letters, the heirs of both sides decided to entrust these documents of fundamental im-

---

[46] Other parts of Michael's legacy are kept in England at the Archives of the Albert Sloman Library, at the University of Essex.

portance to the Österreichische Nationalbibliothek in Vienna, Austria.

Let's not forget that this wealth of archives revealing new and sometimes unexpected material nourished many publications and conferences like the Ferenczi International Conferences. The main ones were: New York 1991;Budapest 1993; Madrid 1998; Turin 2002; London 2003; Baden-Baden 2006; Buenos Aires 2009; Budapest 2013; London 2013; Toronto 2015.

Studying Ferenczi somehow also led me back to our shared original culture, deriving from the time of the Austro-Hungarian Monarchy. The 1980s were characterized by political changes taking place within the Soviet system—the Hungarians cut up the barbed wire on the Austrian border—; Gorbachev wanted something freer and lighter in place of the ruins of the Stalinist order. In the 1980s, when we started working on publishing the correspondence, gaining access to historical and literary documents was, until then, met with the most varied difficulties; often it seemed to be almost impossible. And when we finished the work ten years later, research on the beginning of psychoanalysis was no longer considered a spy activity in Budapest. This was a significant turn, especially for researchers living in that country, and at the same time also a reflection of positive development for the locals, who had suffered a great deal.

It was interesting to experience the possibility that one may even forget one's own mother tongue—in contrast to what is usually asserted in that regard. In 1989, my level of Hungarian was that of a good "hotel language," enough for me to get room and board.

To Ernst: *The cabdriver who took me to my hotel half-turned to me and said: But tell me, sir, where in the world did you learn to speak Hungarian so correctly? In Budapest!, I replied, and I was nearly thrown out of the taxi when he abruptly turned the steering wheel. So surprised was he that I was born there that it could have nearly cost our lives...*

Then I decided to teach seminars on method in Budapest for ten years and spend a weekend in the capital 6–8 times each year.

To Ernst: *I arrived with the feeling that these were not the same kind of psychoanalytic candidates as I knew from Geneva. On the one hand, they were naive, also badly informed about what we call, for lack of anything better, a "real" analysis, on the other hand, they were also somewhat freer from the hierarchical pressure as compared to their candidates in the west. Perhaps I also felt a certain… contempt, or at least a feeling of deficience… But I was very interested. I kept going to Budapest at my own expense, also, to speak the truth, for other reasons, to see my country of origin again after forty years. Several people came to visit my seminars. The older generation in particular observed me, György Vikar and his wife Maria, Lidia Nemes… I wondered whether they wanted to spy, wanted to check if my teaching was really worthwhile, but rather they were honestly interested.*

Ernst: *But it's interesting that you had this feeling.*

André: *We were strangers to each other. This was no real homecoming to me, I had never been an analyst in Budapest, and had never had contact to analysts there, except for those outside the country. At congresses, too, there was little contact. I approached this country with very ambivalent feelings. In other words, there was like a wall between us. But the younger generation and I got to know each other, I came there for supervisions over the weekend eight to ten times a year, and we became closer. I was quite dedicated and very motivated to bring them something. It was not just curiosity; I really got to like them. This was a second phase, which was a very good experience for me. They began to practice what we call "real" analysis; they gave meditative, introjective interpretations in their analyses, they paid attention to the countertransference, etc., and in short they were open to everything I find important. They were very curious, also to read new things. My talks were in Hungarian, a talk at a time, and then they started to read the literature, which was not without difficulties. This country had been famous, partic-*

ularly in my father's generation, for its cultivated and multilingual inhabitants, speaking many languages, above all German and English, but also Italian and French—for instance when my father wanted to welcome my wife he prepared by reading Proust for three days to brush up his French, Proust! But now, people had real difficulties of getting the right books in this country so they could read them. Then, there came a third phase, which was partly in connection with the economic and political situation. They began to get interested in "finally" earning some good money in the capitalist world. As a consequence, certain people switched to pharmacotherapy, and then came all the phenomena we know from our western countries with brief therapies and mixed ones between pharmacological and other methods. I naturally deplored this. They lost rather important and talented people. That's the situation now. It hasn't become a Garden of Eden, although I felt that the younger generation could have developed more enthusiasm and made more discoveries, as is always the case in the beginnings. This impetus soon abated and degraded to this economico-centric routine.

Through discussing cases I re-captured my Hungarian proficiency, which, according to some, I shouldn't have lost to begin with. I know this distancing myself (from bad memories) was necessary, and I have no regrets in this regard. If a multilingual is someone who does not even speak one language properly, then a cosmopolitan is a person who does not consider a single country his home. If he knows languages well, however, he somehow makes every country his home (and this is among the "secondary benefits").

Well, what I have learned from and about Ferenczi—in contrast to others—was not only relational psychoanalysis, but the fact that the relation conceals past events and identifications, as well as experiences of instinctual nature (such as in adolescence). We can learn from Ferenczi, the faithful follower of Freud—Yes, indeed!—see their correspondence—that all these strings can be tied together in order to be able to practice psychoanalysis in a useful and respectable way. I am not a sociable person, rather an individualist. But I value sharing thoughts and experiences with my colleagues. This is why I stayed in the Swiss Society of Psychoanalysis and with it in the International Psychoanalytical Association until today. This is why I joined the Academy of Psychoanalysis founded by Franz Alexander and accepted an honorary membership of the Hungarian, Polish, and German (Deutsche Psychoanalytische Gesellschaft (DPG)) societies. Emotionally, British psychoanalysis is closest to me. Later, I realized that two of the three groups being part of the British Society, in one way or another, originate in Ferenczi. Initially, I was attracted to the middle group, and to some Kleinian ideas, and maybe also to Michael Balint as a person. But other groups, such as the French—from Daniel Lagache to Janine Chasseguet to Michel Fain to Michel Neyraud to Pierre Luquet to Serge Viderman—and important studies by others fundamentally stimulated me.

This is where I would like to say how important international contacts were in my life for understanding psychoanalysis as worldwide phenomena and not just the agglomeration of parochial groups usually around an old man and a woman or women– tied through legal or 'illegal' extra-marital late relationships. A kind of neo-family…

SUPERVISIONS IN THE EUROPEAN WORLD

My travels throughout Europe, which I was solicited to undertake in favor of IPA supervisory activities—to find out whether some new groups were corresponding to the general consensus and regulations of the older established associations–, offered me a wealth of opportunities to consider, examine, evaluate and understand questions tied to convergences and differences. It also and above all gave me occasions for collegial friendships like the ones with Anne-Marie Sandler and John Kafka as well as with many dear German DPG colleagues (Franz Wellendorf, Jürgen Körner, Leila and Ingo Focke, Cornelia Wagner, Bernd and Winnie Gutmann, Thilo Eith, Uschi Kreuzer-Haustein) as well as other German psychoanalysts, especially Carl Nedelmann and Ulrike May, to mention only a few. Moreover, I worked for years with a new Polish group, working under multiple influences (London-Kleinian,

German, French), that formed around Wojtek Hanbowski (after he returned from London) and Katarzyna Walewska (who had trained in Paris), and many others. I cannot mention them all - it would lead me astray.

Outside of any official mission from the IPA, I also worked in regular group supervision with around 15-20 persons in Budapest after the fall of the communist regime over the course of nearly ten years, 6-8 times each year. Most of them have become dear friends over the years. These mutual exchanges between colleagues opened very interesting, and sometimes intriguing, perspectives to me. It became a real learning process, not merely on the margins, but rather in the middle of my and their lives, bringing me also into a whirlwind of other problems, in part, unknown to me until then. Colorful groups of such different personalities...

Encounters with Colleagues in the World

My broad course of teaching and supervisory activities in Europe was happily complemented by unexpected meetings and personal acquaintances with the people who built present-day psychoanalysis.

As psychoanalysis carries imprints of the thinkers who share their experiences with their analytic partners, the magic of the historical study and reading the works of these creative personalities, as well as personal encounters with them, are fundamental to understanding their new ideas and proposals. It is thus that they reveal their processes of unwinding the secrets of their emotions and ideas.

The frail voice of Anna Freud, at once timid and measured; the passion of Ralph Greenson, attacking Kleinism as if it were a criminal conspiracy; the perfect self-mastery of Robert Wallerstein as he proceeded toward a precise goal; the participation of psychologists in professional psychoanalytic organizations; the remarks of Joe Sandler, circumspect, wise advancement, on the subject of theory—all of this in their own timbre, in their way of doing, in their intonation, the strength or weakness of their voice—the collection of all of these elements, and many more still, has again unlocked worlds for me, as much as for identification as for delineation. The complicity of Anne-Marie Sandler's gentleness and inner balance; the intellectual force of Jean Laplanche's well-thought stances; Rudolph Loewenstein's friendliness towards a young analyst at the Congress of Vienna, introduced to him by Raymond de Saussure, was one of those rare encounters about which one can only say: it was an encounter. Heinz Hartman, like Melanie Klein, prominent figures whom I only knew from a distance, but whom I had certainly known beforehand through the accounts of others. All of it came together in a kaleidoscope, not only to help one understand, but also to *experience* the diversity of the personalities, of lives spent in maturing analytic activity. No uniformity whatsoever, and it was better that way.

Figure 27: Anne-Marie and Joe Sandler listening to Paul Parin giving a talk (inauguration of the Psychoanalytic Institute in Geneva, 1973)

These memories evoke others. Very close to me, personally, were my analysts, Paul Parin and Emanuel Windholz, my mentor in the psychoanalytic society, Gustav Bally, and the Faustian personality, Leopold Szondi in Zurich. My winding professional path led me to collaborate intensively with two Genevian colleagues: Raymond de Saussure and Marcelle Spira. It was there as well that I enjoyed the brilliant academic teaching of Julian de Ajuriaguerra. I was inspired by the great inner freedom of Michael Balint and Enid Balint, as well as that of Anne-Marie and Joe Sandler, in London. I became enthusiastic for Donald Winnicott's seminars, Wilfried Bion's lectures, and the artistic baby observer Dan Stern. Jean Laplanche, in Paris, supported me in the publication business. Robert Wallerstein was a protective presence in California…

My life was so full of highly stimulating encounters, exceptional moments which I treasure and which led me to more personal meetings, some of them very impressive, to paths always new and tenderly maintained in the realm of emotional memories of togetherness, closeness, sometimes love. The ones on the shores of the Pacific Ocean, others in other countries and continents—all of them were very important in making me what I have become. Life being an endless process, every impression left its trace and I realize that I am now carefully storing them—in part living from them, exploiting them and using them as mental food to continue to construct what I am.

4

A Psychoanalyst Listening to Fanatics

> *We must, however, acknowledge...that man with all his noble qualities...still bears in his bodily frame the indelible stamp of his lowly origin.*
> CHARLES DARWIN

To Judit: *Another topic followed my concern for depression: it has been a kind of psychological processing of the experiences I'd lived through in Hungary, certain aspects of the Nazi Arrow Cross,[47] and the Stalinist/communist world. The elaboration of this process became a book about fanaticism. It was so significant that I wrote it with another author of Hungarian descent, Miklós Molnár, professor at the Graduate Institute of International and Development Studies in Geneva, and with the collaboration of Parisian anthropologist Gérard de Puymège. Choosing to work with Miklós stemmed from my desire to include somebody with different political ideas. In doing so, I aimed to keep the work at a more scientific, investigatory level, and not let it slide into an ideological discourse.*

Judit: *When did you write your book on fanaticism?*

---

[47] Hitlerist party and movement in Hungary ("Nyilas").

André: A bit later than the one on depression. It was published in French in 1980. Miklós Molnár, was a former communist from the Imre Nagy group, who emigrated to Geneva, became a university professor there, and dealt with nineteenth- and twentieth-century history, mainly that of labor movements and their conflicts. As a result of his former political commitments, he had had the opportunity to study closely the elements of the fanatical mentality.

Judit: How did the project begin?

André: Its genesis was when Saul Friedländer—who was one of the pioneering researchers of the Holocaust and a university professor in Geneva and Jerusalem, at the time, and later in Los Angeles— invited us, Bertrand Cramer and myself, to represent psychoanalysis at regular round table meetings that he organized. Miklós Molnár was also part of it. Friedländer later, independently from us, wrote his own book stimulated, in part, by our discussions. After the round table, Miklós and I continued our exchanges and were later joined by Gérard de Puymège. We deliberated about life in totalitarian systems and tried to understand "them" (the fanatics) and our own reactions. Mólnar's knowledge enlarged our perspective. For example, he even reached back in his study to the notorious Tiszaeszlár[48] trial as one of the first traumatic manifestations provoked by Hungarian anti-Semitism at the end of the nineteenth century.... Until then, over the centuries, Christian and Jewish Hungarians had co-existed without problems (Fejtö, 1997) (the country had never had ghettos prior to German occupation in 1944). Preparing the book, our conversations were rich and touched on the range of fanatic ideologies and their appeal to masses at different points of history.

---

[48] Comparable in its symbolic meaning to the Dreyfuss trial in France, in this Hungarian town a famous trial took place: Jews were accused of having killed a young Christian girl in order to use her blood for Jewish rituals of rejuvenation. The trial ended not only with the acquittal of the Jews, but also with the condemnation of the anti-Semitic rumormongers.

Once it came out, our book was snapped up in the stores with unprecedented speed. The preeminent Parisian newspaper "Le Monde" covered it on the front page and then, out of the blue, it fell victim to communist manipulation and all but disappeared from the shop windows.

Figure 28: «Fanaticism» book review on the title page of Le Monde

Judit: How did that happen?

André: Bernard Pivot, the big star of book reviews on French television, had me on and we spoke about the topic for two hours. So if I want to show off with that book, well, at first, it was a big success.... However, the French communist party decided that the concept of 'totalitarianism'—which derived primarily from Hannah Arendt— did not exist at all. But if it existed, then it could only be false and deceitful because, for them, it conflated communism with Nazism.

Today, the term has made its way into mainstream political science but at the time the communist parties were fighting what is now its mostly accepted use.

Judit: So it was subject to major criticism?

André: ... from the communist side because it compromised the communist doctrine. After the huge initial promotion, the book disappeared in France—but there were later Israeli and American editions, both from the same publisher. It sold well and had a certain impact.

Judit: What challenges did it pose as you were working on it?

André: For me, the point was to understand how fanatics could have gone so far. This is the question we all asked: how could people have come to such degrading regimes—I'd prefer not to call them "vile," but certainly subhuman and cruel. How could those degrading totalitarian regimes develop in the twentieth century in what had been the Germany of Beethoven and Goethe or in the Soviet Union of Tolstoy, Dostoyevsky and Gorky? And then, after '68, I had the sense that something else had started, a new perspective; the concept of "political correctness" was not always the same as simple "ethical correctness" (e.g., "Don't kill, Don't torture"). It carried with itself a political conviction without sufficient explicit and clear reference to ethics, for example the request for an abolition of inheritance, even the small values of modest earners. The communists sensed very keenly that the notion of political correctness could advance their cause, so we had to watch where it all might lead. Because, you know, even certain deeply harmful processes always start with the best intentions....

A friend of mine from the United States' west coast, asked me once, with surprise, why I am so preoccupied with politics.

Well, indeed I have dealt with politics and history a lot in my life, as they determined my fate to a large extent all the way to the end of the 1950s, and again recently. I meditated extensively about this personal history. This led me to write about fanaticism then and now these lines here.

Naturally, I also stumbled upon the Irrational in fanaticism. To the question already so frequently raised after World War II, "How could all of this have happened?" we often only received general one-size-fits-all responses. There was, however, not one effective recipe against its repetition in sight. Disappointment followed "victory" at the end of the war, and our fast-paced society shifted to another, primarily economic, model of interpretation of these wartime destructions, although one model (economic, like German war industry's interests) does not exclude the other (psychological, like fanaticism and political revanchism), and the interplay of various factors should obviously be considered.[49]

Isn't the best way to reflect about this subject to explore what two big thinkers of our modern time have written about it? I begin my thoughts with them.

CIVILIZATIONS AND THEIR ILLUSIONS

> *Nothing is more sad than the death of an illusion.*
> ARTHUR KOESTLER

In 1932, Albert Einstein asked Sigmund Freud, "Is there any way of delivering mankind from the menace of war? ... How is it these devices [schools, the press, and the Church, usually under the influence of the ruling class] succeed so well in rousing men to such wild enthusiasm, even to sacrifice their lives?" (Einstein, in: Freud 1933b, p. 199 &sqq).

In his response to Einstein, and in other key writings in the 1920s, Freud dealt in depth with the issues of civilization and their illusions. In his long answer to Einstein he states that getting rid of men's aggressive inclinations is an impossible endeavor. However, if there is one, culture is the antidote. All that we can achieve to foster civilization will contribute in preventing war.

---

[49] For the psychoanalytic contributions, see the works of Vamik D. Volkan and the investigations of Alexander Mitscherlich and, later, Cornelius Castoriadis, to name a few.

Following in his footsteps, I examined this weighty question in our contemporary world. This I did, motivated by the fact that, when I was 14 years old, I was struck by war and foreign occupation, which brought with them the persecutions which I describe earlier, like Uncle Teddy who had to stay hidden and my cousins who disappeared to the Siberian camps. I simply cannot forget.

The phenomenon of fanaticism, sadly, determined the history of the twentieth century in a profound and fundamental way. The beginning of the twenty-first century is no more promising. The largest populations since World War II have had to leave their homes and countries; the total destruction of cities and villages threaten us with a horrible repetition of history. Fanaticism has permeated a great many aspects of life down to the most trivial, everyday elements; buying or obtaining basic needs like water and food exposes many to the risk of arrest or capture.

Fanaticism didn't disappear in the period after the Second World War and it infiltrated the otherwise seemingly peaceful life of the 50 years that followed. In spite of the terrible devastation of the European continent, it emerged periodically in public life in the most varied forms—nationalism, chauvinism, religious and political fundamentalism, as well as in the form of utopian, sectarian pseudo-religions.

What strikes the psychoanalyst in the fanatical discourse is a frequent emergence of the notion of enemy, malfeasance, evil, and, overall, of a world of persecution. This reveals an extreme sense of danger. If Freud and other pioneers of psychoanalysis sought to understand the crises of the Victorian Era, then it falls to our generation and the next one to confront the problems and divisions of the civilizations of our day.

What protects the current or future fanatic in this "terrible world" is the feeling of security against the forces of evil, which mustn't have the last word. This false sense of security is solely based either on the assurances of a divinity derived from certain forms of religiosity or on a certain interpretation of the sciences. The sciences have shaped themselves to become the religion of our time, basing their prestige and authority on an apparently validated knowledge. It is also supposed that they enlighten the obscurities of social life, and these suppositions have transformed into ideologies that underpin movements such as Marxism,

Zionism, nationalism, spiritualism, New Age-ism, and in various forms of politico-religious movements. The promise of these ideologies is the utopia of finding the right path to a better future, made possible by the metaphorical birth of a new human being—the true communist, the genuine patriot, or the zealot. The new Man, new country, or new life promises complete happiness. The world of the fanatic is composed, on the one hand, of the projection of horrible scapegoats and, on the other hand, of idealized all-good contents. There is no middle ground, no discussion of facts: there is no way to approach reality, to recognize its existence. It is a world of fairy tales and terrible menaces.

So these behaviors lead to the birth of closed political ideologies, disregarding a critical analysis of facts in order to thus maintain the belief system. As T. S. Eliot concluded, "Humankind cannot bear very much reality."[50]

WHAT ACCOUNTS FOR THE APPEAL OF FANATICISM?

Fanaticism is based on a system of thought which, in the name of a divinity, a nation, or any other power that represents unquestionable authority—including the authority of modern science—claims itself to be the repository of the sole, exclusive truth: "Things are like this or like that, and that cannot be questioned because it is God's revelation!" or "Things are like this or like that, and that cannot be questioned since science has 'proved it'!" Dogmatism of this sort inevitably leads to a narcissistic self-righteousness and a seemingly unshakable, elitist self-confidence: "We are the keepers of truth." Such an exclusive attitude unconditionally demands a sacrifice of reason on the altar of belief, as Tertullian's famous formula also bears witness: "Credo quia absurdum [I believe because it is absurd]." Any doubt, any possibility of further questioning and rational analysis of external and internal realities are, by definition, ruled out, leading to ignorance, to the extent of intellectual self-mutilation and great loss inflicted on the individual and society.

Fanaticism succeeds as long as the "empire" built upon it exists, and until the construction falls in the wake of either a cataclysmic war or a

---

[50] T. S. Eliot (1888 – 1965) "Four Quartets".

destructive economic crisis—as happened with Hitler's and Stalin's empires. Fanatical dictatorships like these came to a horrible end not all that long ago, notably in Serbia and Romania and in the Arab and Middle Eastern countries in the 20th and 21st centuries. The devastating power of fanaticism is demonstrated in numerous other examples, notably in the terrible events taking place in Syria nowadays.

In contemporary terrorism, fanaticism found a fertile soil for an overflowing movement with a radicalization of its ideology—"Do not kill" is no longer respected, and neither is the prohibition of cruelties like torture—and has become solidified through the confluence of different influences. Beyond the security of religious doctrine, it may also offer a way of life to youths. While the fanatic movements behind the fanaticism were often only a secondary phenomenon in the life of the individual, these new, young fanatic-terrorists receive a lifestyle that is rewarded, practically as a professional fanatic. Their recruitment takes into account their circumstances, an existence otherwise stripped of hope, and promises them a total separation from their grim and undesirable social and family histories and a true sense of purpose.

OBJECTIONS

A frequent objection to a psychological approach to fanaticism consists of the reminder that it can only be interpreted against the background of a specific cultural context. But it should be considered that, nevertheless, all our cultures generally tended to make murder taboo. It is thus legitimate and valuable to examine the personality structure of offenders, for example, murderers, from the perspective of psychology, that is, from the perspective of a contemporary acquired knowledge.

But why and how a mentality, an internal connection that may be called pre-fanatical, develops in an individual and spills over into open fanaticism in particular historical, social, and economic situations? Nowadays, we are all confronted with fanatics in the media and are puzzled by the phenomenon. How is this possible? What might prompt someone to embrace such extreme views? Some answers may lie in studies of past fanatic movements. For example studies on Nazism—i.e., the writings of Hannah Arendt—have demonstrated that those who served the system were, for the most part, everyday people who had become devout, blind servants to fanatical purposes, organized into the infantry of the dictatorship.

The Structure of Fanaticism, from its Birth on

First of all, let us consider the role of the "original fanatic," the figure of the initiator, the innovator, the originator. Frequently, he creates a new philosophy, establishes a new religion (or at least thoroughly transforms a previously existing religious tradition, as with ISIS), or develops a political ideology that promises universal happiness. The disseminators of these ideas present themselves in the public eye as the keepers of the ultimate truth. They refer to a truth that is usually in their exclusive possession, either as a result of some divine revelation or on the basis of "indisputable" scientific findings (like the use of genetics and "race" in the Nazi ideology). Frequently, a charismatic person grabs fleeting ideas and presents them as new perspectives; the possibility of doubt or criticism is foredoomed to exclusion in these cases. With his gestures and personal magnetism, he practically embodies the truth he advocates—a truth that has the power to fanaticize others—and he identifies with it to the extent that he embraces it without any criticism. Indeed, so lacking in criticism is he that he is willing to stand by it until the fateful fall. Hitler stood by his insane obstinacy until his suicide, Beria until his execution, and Stalin until the murder that ultimately ended his life (supposedly, no one dared go to the aid of the dying dictator for two days).

We can round out the anatomy of fanaticism with a few more elements, one of them being the technique of creating a scapegoat: "Everything is someone else's fault;" "We are innocent;" "We are not responsible for anything." Another feature of fanaticism can be found in group dynamics (which I elaborate in a later section).

Members fully submit themselves to the rules and regulations of the organization and subordinate their own will to the unquestionable authority of the leader. Members have the utmost loyalty to one another based on shared convictions. Members, the believers, are, at best, neutral towards outsiders—the infidels, the right-wingers, the left-wingers—but it is even better if they express hostile feelings toward them. And, finally, in return for the grace of being chosen and initiated into the ultimate truth, they submit, in order to further the achievement of the great goal, with their whole lives to bring to victory the true cause, to realize the official objectives of the party or the cult. Frequently, literature manages to portray the basic features of human existence very perceptively. In Gulliver's Travels, Swift describes the bloody war that broke out between the Lilliputians and the Blefuscudians over the proper way to crack open a soft-boiled egg. 11,000 people fell victim to this war. They had rather choose death than submit, crack their eggs open on the narrow end, and thus forsake their identity.

SIMPLIFIED WORLD

From the perspective of the individuals—the fanaticized—, who are being appealed to by the charismatic person, the ideology offers a way out or a better reality. Fanaticism transports the individual to a simplified world, and thus he experiences a regression of consciousness.

The simplifying ideology that projects the perfect future becomes fertile soil for fanatical needs. Such an ideology is quickly able to satisfy our fanatical longing for simple solutions.

The greater the theoretical uncertainty, the more questionable the facts are, the more questions there are that are impossible to resolve, the stronger the drive becomes towards fanatical blindness. Moreover, the community of friends and comrades that is forged through a mutually recognized truth, the closed group that is protective and spares one the hardships of the external world, has a galvanizing and fanaticizing effect in and of itself.

As I have noted earlier, fanaticism is rooted in a philosophy which claims to be the repository of a sole, exclusive truth, through reference to divine revelation or some other similarly unquestionable authority (nowadays, in our culture, this is primarily the authority of simplified "science"). The illusion that the philosopher's stone or the master key has been discovered leads, in most cases, to boundless conceit. We can justifiably call this conceit "narcissistic" because it is through it that the individual considers himself to be among the "chosen" ones. In possession of the ultimate truth, the individual may imagine himself to be an "Übermensch," a superhuman, exceptional and superior to others. The illusion of the final truth—which is, in most cases, some one-sided half-truth—that dominates over everything, creates a stupefying false sense of superiority. Any objection can be dismissed: in fanatical religions, this is called the sacrifice of the intellect (sacrificium intellectus).[51] Closed political ideologies, for example, certain extreme versions of Marxism (e.g., Stalinism and Pol Pot-ism), similarly disregard a critical, rational analysis of reality in order to maintain their own belief system. Findings from empirical sciences have often been rejected in the name of unquestionable authority or religious considerations (e.g., Galileo) or because of their incompatibility with the political doctrine (such as the views on genetics in Nazi Germany and USSR, psychology in the Soviet Union and nowadays against climate change). However, with overheated emotions, other types of ideas may be suitable for representation as an ideological panacea, as magic that offers a solution to everything.

Messianism, eschatology, and various utopias represent creations from the same mentality. Messianism is based on the belief that the Messiah will return now or in the near future and transform the world to its origins, a belief which has existed from early on in the Jewish tradition and can be found in the Christian Bible as well; eschatology means waiting for the near apocalypse; and millenarianism is a hope for the imminent establishment of a thousand-year reign. There also exists a secular tradition of the perfect reign, earthly paradise: utopianism. St. Augustine theorized on the perfect state as early as the fifth century, a tradition that Thomas More revived and transformed at the end of the eighteenth century through the concept of utopia (from the Greek ou (οὐ) "no" and topos (τόπος) "place"), that is, "Noplace." Even today, a similar utopianism urges the fanatical fundamentalist to commit a suicide attack with the promise of entering the heavenly realm, paradise. For instance, followers of the Rev.

---

[51] See Loyola as well as Blaise Pascal and Kierkegaard.

Jim Jones, who committed mass suicide, were also victims of fanaticism (inexplicably, over 900 believers ended their lives at the same time in the jungles of Guyana), just like members of a Swiss cult whose lives also ended in a mass suicide (in the latter case, the number of victims was lower perhaps because Switzerland has fewer inhabitants, and the cult had smaller numbers.) Nor was the Ayatollah Khomeini's bloody Islamic Revolution any less fanatical: music was forbidden, as were public baths for both sexes, and it was declared that homosexuals be persecuted. Excessive asceticism and Puritanism are often inspired by fanatic influences. Moreover, hostile discrimination towards women was also part of this issue. All this shows a deep suspicion of basic instincts, which is often characteristic of fanaticism.

However horrible all of this may be, as long as we are not talking about the personal life of one or the other, then even people outside the fanatic group would rather close their eyes resignedly over the horrors or make any effort not to notice them at all, unfortunately, as a psychic self-protection. This contributes to the spreading of fanatic ideology.

Everyday Fanaticism

Fanaticism is the contrary of tolerance, empathy and understanding of the others.

Besides great historical movements, "everyday fanaticism" also exists: the fanaticism of day-to-day life. Consider the type of fanaticism that arises within the family: "I know what's right," a father or mother, a daughter or son affirms. "If we structure our lives according to my truth, we will soon be blessed with heavenly peace and happiness here in the family." The people around us can consider their own view as the only right perspective and will try to impose it, they will not admit the other's opinions, thus having trouble integrating and participating in a shared endeavor.

At work a "fanatic" colleague in a hierarchically higher position will impose his own ideas, convinced that they are "right", that they don't need to be confronted with those of others nor negotiated; this boss will not consult with his/her team. Even authoritarian bosses on the other hand can be prepared to revise their ideas, and so avoid becoming fanatic. A fanatic subordinate will have difficulties submitting to colleagues' requests, thinking that they are erroneous and that he, himself, has the only appropriate ideas… he will suffer considerably at his workplace and have the hardest time collaborating.

Although we will discuss this topic later in more detail, let me remark that psychoanalysis has also, without a doubt, run the risk of becoming a utopian ideology, which as early as the 1960s was sometimes called "psychoanalism." This ideology offered the unshakable conviction of not only being in the right, but also holding the Truth with no possibility of error. If somebody doesn't accept psychoanalytic theses it is "purely because of affective resistances" (considered in this system as a "sin" would be in a religious context). The inherent complexities of the natural sciences, the limitations of the transformational power of psychoanalysis, did not stand in the way of these simplistic convictions.

Sometimes, in some psychoanalytically inspired groups, thinking can be abused into considering human frailties as "evidently (morally) bad" and be wildly interpreted outside any therapeutic setting as neurotic. For example, a man who bites his nails could be thought of as an "eater of his own body" by onlookers who consider themselves (falsely) to be "enlightened by psychoanalytic science"!

Members of a Cult

We also encounter fanaticism among our patients in clinical practice; indeed, I myself have had the opportunity to work with fanatics and cult members. I felt that I had been carried off to another world where the members resembled each other in their mental construction through their beliefs. Those constructions explain the unshakable adherence to the fanatical systems. Generally, it takes a dramatic and spectacular confrontation to put an end to the utopias.

These sets of beliefs, fed by (sometimes sadistic) emotions or impulses, only falter when an external reality destroys whatever credibility remains of the fanatical system. The collapse of false beliefs is provoked either on the political-historical level by wars, uprisings, revolutions, economic defeats, or similar impactful negative societal events or in other areas by radical changes in the scientific views that laid the foundation for the ideology in question.

The psychoanalyst's work brings to light deep emotional psychological forces and repressed passions that underlie relatively simple mechanisms. These passions are strongly reinforced and favored by certain socio-economic circumstances that enable them to predominate. The particular combination of those forces, i.e., of a particular psychology, as examined above, and of a certain socio-economic situation, feeds the fierceness with which fanatics hang on to their convictions.

By allowing insights about the disastrous effects of fanaticism, psychoanalysis offers the analysand a reflection on the psychic functioning of both the fanatical individual himself and his or her group. In contrast, soft illusions, as are encountered in the arts or in some milder forms of historical religions, are quite different from malignant utopias.

Moreover, the Freudian theories related to destructiveness contribute to a better understanding of these phenomena. Even the psychoanalytical community was reluctant to accept the importance of destructive forces, as Freud himself bears witness in *Civilization and its Discontents*: "... an instinct of... destruction has met with resistance even in analytic circles..." (Freud 1930a, p. 119); and "It is clearly not easy for men to give up the satisfaction of this inclination to aggression. They do not feel comfortable without it. The advantage which a comparatively small... group offers of allowing this instinct an outlet in the form of hostility against intruders is not to be despised" (Freud 1930a, p. 114).

At an advanced stage of psychotherapy, a particular patient of mine begged me to acknowledge that everything he had done in his position of power during his country's dictatorship had been right and justified, at least under the prevailing conditions of the time. He begged me to acknowledge that the crimes that now weighed on his conscience had been committed then and there in the service of justice. It is clear that he was clinging tenaciously to this last illusion before he was able to let his former fanatical convictions go. The depression that followed was the price he paid, and it could only be overcome through a long period of introspection...

I would like to share two short quotations from Freud: one is a rather gloomy commentary, and the other is a conclusion in the spirit of greater promise. Let us begin with the bad news, the pessimistic consideration: "The fateful question for the human species seems to me to be whether and to what extent their cultural development will succeed in mastering the disturbance of their communal life by the human instinct of aggression and self-destruction. It may be that in this respect precisely the present time deserves a special interest. Men have gained control over the forces of nature to such an extent that with their help they would have no difficulty in exterminating one another to the last man. They know this, and hence comes a large part of their current unrest, their unhappiness and their mood of anxiety. And now it is to be expected that the other of the two 'Heavenly Powers', eternal Eros, will make an effort to assert himself in the struggle with his equally immortal adversary. But who can foresee with what success and with what result?" (Freud 1930a, p. 145). These are impressive lines that demonstrate important foresight, considering that Freud wrote them twelve years before the birth of the nuclear menace.

Let us therefore hope that the more optimistic Freud will carry the day over the uncertain and pessimistic one. He also said: "The voice of the intellect is a soft one, but it does not rest till it has gained a hearing. Finally, after a countless succession of rebuffs, it succeeds" (Freud 1927c, p. 53). It is up to us to make the voice of intellect audible in our world.

The fanatical attitude promises a great deal and holds out the promise of so many good and "positive" things. But what an enormous price to be paid for fanatical obsessions and what destruction they cause! That price should not be paid again. Moreover, it is in fact our professional and human obligation to remain sensitive and vigilant to this dangerous phenomenon. It is a poor excuse to say that we have encountered relatively few fanatics during our therapeutic activities. First, there are many members of cults who end up seeing us psychologists and psychiatrists. Second, when we say that, we are disregarding what are called "formes frustes", that is, cases of latent, hardly-manifested fanatics.

Generally speaking, we must aim at broadening the complex intellectual horizon of our profession and at the same time act as responsible citizens and, indeed, decent people in our society.

André E. Haynal

THE FANATICS AND THEIR GROUP

Figure 29: Sigmund Freud's Conference about Fanaticism

Freud, has opened yet another door: his insights remind us that in life one is "part of a group" and society (Freud, 1927c, 1930a). In fact, the individual behaves differently in groups and comes to feel, think, and act in a manner entirely different under its influence. "It would be obliged to explain the surprising fact that under a certain condition, this individual, whom it had come to understand, thought, felt and acted in quite a different way from what would have been expected. And this condition is his insertion into a collection of people which has acquired the characteristic of a 'psychological group'. " (Freud, 1921c, p. 72)

When we examine the fanatic individually, we neglect the group he/she belongs to. Freud partly anticipated what Ferenczi and Winnicott later wrote, i.e. that the "natural" state of human being is to be part of a group, and individual psychology is only a theoretical abstraction.

His text on "group psychology" (1921c) falls midway between the *Three Essays* (1905d) and *Instincts and their Vicissitudes* (1915c) and the great works on culture and civilization, *The Future of an Illusion* (1927c), *Civilization and its Discontents* (1930a), etc. In retrospect, after a century of manmade disasters, it is all the more necessary to listen more carefully to his message.

Since his writings, fanaticism holds a prominent position in the world. How can psychoanalysis contribute to shedding light on it, particularly along the path that Freud set with his 1921 work: *Group psychology and the analysis of the Ego*?

Let us first remember the importance of the ego ideal in this text. It explains a wide range of phenomena including romantic obsession with or dependence on a hypnotizing charismatic personality, fascination, even submission to an abusive and powerful leader, like Hitler. As a last resort, the text was a political work that sprang forth after the First World War, but particularly following the dissolution of the Danubian monarchy, which made Freud—along with many of his collaborators who, like Freud, came from the peripheral regions of the empire—lose his rootedness in the homelands of his ancestors. "Little Austria" was born, and Freud exclaimed: "It is painful to think that more or less the whole world will be a foreign country" (correspondence to Ferenczi, March 17, 1919). Before that, turn-of-the-century Vienna, under the reign of Francis-Joseph I, had been not only a theatre of exceptional cultural, scientific, and artistic explosion, but also a place where the ideals of pluralism, tolerance, and multilingualism came to life in the Eastern part of Europe– even if they did so imperfectly. This Vienna was the home of Freud, to which he was attached—albeit in an ambivalent manner. Group psychology and the analysis of the Ego was, without any doubt, one step in his grieving process. The grieving process aroused in him an effort of understanding. He said in a letter to Romain Rolland (March 4, 1923): "Not that I consider this writing to have especially succeeded, but it demonstrates the way that leads from the analysis of the individual toward the comprehension of society" (Vermorel and Vermorel, 1993, p. 219). Note that in Freud's original title of his text, the word "Massen," the masses, was translated in English as Group. The text by Gustave Le Bon, The Crowd: A study of the popular mind (1895), on which Freud relied, spoke of "the masses" as well, not of groups. Le Bon examined the relationship of the crowd to the leader—which also means, when taken to one extreme, the relationship between the fanaticizer and the fanaticized. He also notices the existence of a feeling of hostility, even hatred, towards those who are not members of the group and, as such, represent a danger to the cohesion of the group. Furthermore, the concepts of instincts, of "identification," the "differentiation of the Ego," the "ego ideal," allow us to examine the phenomena of social life, particularly fanaticism. Jacques Lacan, in The Situation of Psychoanalysis and the Training of the Psychoanalyst (1956), directs our attention to the fact that Freud just anticipated fascist organizations, and Jean-Bertrand Pontalis spoke of a "primary psychological explanation—anticipated—of Nazism" (Pontalis, 1968). If this is true, it is also true that at the same time that Freud drafted his text, the Soviet Union's Bolshevik regime was being established, and the clerical organization in Austria, particularly the clerical semi-fascism of the 1930s of Chancellors Dollfuss and Schuschnigg (cf. Wenninger, Dreidemy, 2013), had begun to cast its shadow.

Changes in history condition psychic changes: at a large scale we speak of alterations in mentality. At the level of the individual, these modifications manifest in their 'ego ideal,' which would, in turn, have a direct impact on their actions. In historical situations, their feelings, their identity could end up with identity gaps, or a void, a lack, which, depending on the season in their life, would call loudly to be met by different internal movements. Otherwise, the individual could be drawn into an anti- or a-social identity that threatens exclusion from the contemporary accepted social order and into inclusion in smaller, marginal groups. These compensating groups are mostly recruited from among a psychologically or materially poorer milieu, prone to alternative thinking or to a more extreme form of the dominant ideology.

Despite the apparent differences, a study of Hungary, the relatively small central European country, and the larger Turkey reveals striking parallels, and both countries illustrate this well. First, both countries were part of an empire: Hungary until 1919 at the abdication of the last Kaiser and Turkey until 1924, when the last Islamic empire ended after over 600 years of domination in the region. The end of a theological and political sovereignty and the creation, in turn, of a secular state in Turkey happened in parallel to the end of Hungary's Catholic monarchy, which evolved slowly into its eventual replacement by a secular conception of the "state." These political changes accompanied a pronounced decline in power for the Hungarian part of the Hapsburg Empire and similarly for the Turkish part of the Ottoman Empire: each of these "new" countries saw their former territories and their regional power decrease significantly. In Hungary it gave way to the adoption of nostalgic identities such as the *irredenta*, the order of the 'vitéz' (braves) who took on traditional clothing (called 'Bocskay'), and particularly the old nobility who embraced the slogan, "No, no never!", in support of a semi-dictator and old officer of the defunct empire. In Turkey, it led to the creation of the Muslim Brotherhood in 1928, which fiercely mourned the decline of political Islam.

For these latter, it marked the reestablishment of the caliphate through the defeat of the (post)-colonial system; for those former, it marked the resurrection of the Greater Hungary, one thousand years in existence, thanks to Hitler's intervention (restituting to Hungary some of those territories that belonged to it prior to the Treaty of Versailles). Both mentalities carry with them the memory of trauma and undeniable organizational and economic collapse. In the two countries, the elites were on the road to accept basic ideas of the Enlightenment and political emancipation, contrary to the dominant conservative forces demanding, respectively, the restoration of the Islamist theological system and of a "Christian national" system (*magyar keresztény - nemzeti*) in Hungary. To be, first and foremost, Muslim—or to be, first and foremost, Magyar-Christian—introduces comparable mentalities. Without the ideological incentive to conceive the necessary reforms (for example, agrarian in Hungary, or commercial and industrial in the ex-caliphate), both systems fell into hardship, even to the verge of ruin.

Of course, in both systems, there remain "believers," "true believers," even "truer believers," and then "fanatics," ready to kill the infidels, the enemies. They consider these to be the former masses of immigrants, in the ex-Hapsburg Empire which encompass Jews from western Poland and Lithuania, Germanic peoples from the westernmost territories like Swabia, Armenians and gypsies, among others, from the east of Hungary.

Between those who are wholly true Muslim and all sorts of other Islamists, there would be fewer differences than between "true Magyars" and others for whom it would not be possible to adopt such an identity. Those who are not "in" (included) remain "outside," citizens who "came after," the "un-rooted" Hungarians. The extremists become even more extreme, suicide bombers. In Hungary, the far-rightist Hitlerians ("nyilas"), enraged by their defeat in 1944, ignited the whole country in order to destroy everything and did not refrain from killing "racially" discriminated populations with their firearms, sometimes at point-blank. As within sects, the blend of myth and reality created a mixed composition that served to construct and maintain toxic identities. Neither in Hungary, nor in Turkey did the nostalgia for an idealized, unreal, a-historic past disappear. The official policy of both countries advocated a return to some forms of this past. It is said that, in Hungary, they only celebrate the memory of defeats. The nation bears the sentiment of eternal loser. In Turkey, the nostalgia for an Islamic cultural heritage has not easily found its legitimate expression. The creation of a comfortable world, freer and fairer, seems to be reserved only for other countries and other peoples, while at the same time, the true believers continue to demonize these "un-believers."

OUTLOOK ON OUR EPOCH

After the killings of over 40 million, Arthur Koestler (1978) keenly observed that the twentieth century had spawned Hitlerism, Stalinism, and Maoism, while the sixth century B.C. had witnessed the flowering of Taoism, Confucianism, and Buddhism. According to Haldane (1932), fanaticism first emerged in our culture sometime between 3000 and 1400 B.C. The prophetic religions (Judaism, Christianity, and Islam) emerged each as repositories of a sole, exclusive truth, and it was presumably this set of circumstances that prompted the rise of fanaticism. In contrast, Hinduism and Buddhism are far less dogmatic on basic questions of human existence and allow a great deal more room for ambivalence about human existence.

Freud, in studying the Church, as he knew it –the Catholic variation of Christianity that was birthed out of the Counter-Reformation and sustained by the House of Hapsburg –, clearly analyzed the forces that intertwined to create these phenomena.

Can psychoanalysis contribute to the understanding of these deeds, which have for so long poisoned our culture and our civilization? Can it illuminate the foundations within the individual psyche of the forces that drive man—perhaps even each one of us—to become fanatic?

It has taken a long time for us to recognize the importance of this phenomenon and its destructive power. Excluding a few enlightened minds, such as Erasmus and Spinoza, practically no one paid it heed before the Enlightenment. The notion of fanaticism is thus inextricably tied to the European culture of the past few centuries. The "philosophes" of the eighteenth century were the first to address it more directly. The term was used initially in denouncing religious zealotry. It is the antinomy of Enlightenment, of Reason—it points ultimately in the opposite direction of tolerance, pluralism, and freedom of thought. The origin of "fanaticism" is found in the word *fanum*, meaning "temple," and denounces anything that could be excessive, extravagant, within the context of participation in a religion or a form of religion that one would now call "fundamentalist."

This religion, which the philosophes and Voltaire tended to denounce, the Christian religion in its Catholic form as it belonged to the cardinals and their allies in the French monarchy, is the same one that invented the Inquisition within Europe and the vastly destructive missions to other, outside civilizations. In the periods of progressive loss of faith that followed, it espoused the great secular religions and all kinds of utopias as being the fruition of the Kingdom of God here, on earth: Chauvinism as nationalism, Hitler's National Socialism, the Stalin-Mao-Pol Pot brands of communism, etc. Finally, these new forms of religiosity have reproduced their fanatic expression, most notably in the different sects which continued to propagate even toward the end of our last century, after the fall of these different secular doctrines (such as Nazism and communism).

What is the reason for the call so striking, the seduction so profound, that emanates from fanaticism? As it is built on an intellectual system that declares itself in possession of a sole and unique Truth, such affirmations allow for a narcissistic self-exaltation, or even an enormous security.

In other terms, one removes by force all doubt, all potential for questioning or the emergence of any new perspective. Otherwise put, any possible analysis of reality (external or internal). This makes up part of what fanaticism represents as a possible loss for the individual and for society. In a fanatical society, one no longer considers reality, but remains fanatic until the collapse, until the flames of war or economics destroy the "Empire" based on fanaticism (for example, those of Hitler, Stalin, or the nationalistic versions of Bosnia, Kosovo, and others). The absurd genocide of millions of Cambodians, massacred by the Khmer Rouge in the name of a mystical "clean slate"—initially for the construction of an elusive utopia—; the first model of "ethnic cleansing" in our modern history was perpetrated against the Armenians; the excesses of the French Revolution which would destroy Lyon simply because it was not "Jacobian" enough: all of this gives testimony to this crushing force, as well as to the harmfulness, even the destructiveness of the emotional short-circuiting of problems that deserve to be analyzed and resolved by rational means. Things become simple in the regressive state of the fanatic; there is the "good" and the "bad", we are the good ones, the elect; the bad ones are the others, because they do not believe what we say.

A Manichean division of the world into good and evil, a reduction of the polyphonic to the unison, was often present in religious discourse: the Christian tradition of Civitas Dei, St. Augustine's Kingdom of Heaven versus the pagan "World," is one example which has persisted in all Christian traditions, be they Catholic or Reformed.

This intellectual structure, however—it is already clear from the preceding—cannot exist without the powerful, affective forces that support it. It is there that Freud made us understand that the identification with the leader, the near-hypnotic submission to his voice, the projection of all of our hopes and all of our ideals onto him, are the beginning of a process that allows us to stand among the "good" ones, the Just, according to the immense—or, so to speak, supernatural—wisdom of the leader. Whether this is, once again, in the name of divinity or in the name of science or in the presupposed genius of this leader, the band of brothers finds itself safe and secure. No more doubt, no more questioning, no more intellectual or other effort, it's the solution that promises paradise—be it on earth (as in the various "utopianisms") or in the Hereafter (as in the religious forms).

This distancing from reality can take on its own form of excess. The identity of the individual is called into question so much that any challenge of this identity or its justification arouses self-defensive aggressiveness—in our language, of the aftermath following the initial trigger of narcissistic injuries and of elements invested in the image of the self—and brings about phenomena of extraordinary violence. Entire countries engulfed by flames and blood, countless masses annihilated, just as in the historical religious wars—humanity's most horrific wars—as well as the history of the twentieth century with its secular religions, demonstrate just that.

The Initiator and the Follower

How are these fanatic phenomena born out of the course of history, how do they take shape? It is in this context that Bolterauer's (1975) distinction between "original fanatic" or "fanaticizer" and "induced fanatic" takes on meaning. The fanaticizer, from whom the fanatic idea arises or who is among the first to have succumbed, in an almost religious-like conversion, to the fanatic quality of the idea, induces others to capitulate to the same fanatical state of mind. Thus, the idea not only becomes permissible or plausible—and does not solely trigger, as we have said, almost self-defensive aggressions (defending the fragile narcissism vested in the idea, the leader, or the fanatical group) but also lifts the last inhibitions imposed by the cultural Superego of their environment, the prevailing and educating traditions. The revolt against an unsatisfying state that can very well exist—and the search anew for a perfect state, following the emotional appeals of the fanaticizer, allow the suppression of the Superego (Rangell, 1974). Because of the legitimizing rationalization of the moral transgression (for example: "It is for the good of humanity that we kill"), the "righteous" man, according to the perspective of the fanaticizing idea, can not only succumb to an incredible megalomania (Hitler) or suffer the consequences of such in the form of paranoid persecution (Stalin), but also transgresses any taboo determined by the

Superego or the ego ideal. The Oedipal frustrations, the subsequent grieving processes (Chasseguet-Smirgel, 1975) are short-circuited by deeds, the perverse solutions now legitimized by the fanaticizing idea. Wilhelm Reich (1933) has already described the dynamic of the man who cannot accept his fundamental nature and tries to rid himself of it by attributing it to the Jews, gypsies, Muslims, the rapacious and greedy bourgeois, thus relegating to the exterior that which belongs to his own self: a fundamental nature full of sexual and aggressive desires—but which can be removed thanks to fanatic projections.

Throughout history, the success of fanaticism is naturally also tied to the state of society. The messianic speech of a fanaticizer only carries if it is met by expectation in the miserable state of society, be it economic or in its ideals, in its faith and in its acceptance—and subject, for some authors, to potential self-fanaticization. Max Weber's theory of charisma (1947) and Gustave Le Bon's theory of prestige (1895) try to comprehend the mysterious power held by the leaders of masses—of which the most perfect example, for both authors, is Napoleon—to captivate and, at the same time, paralyze the judgment of others. Let us not forget that the legitimacy of Mohammed rests entirely upon the immediate relationship—without any intermediary—that he held with the Ineffable, with God. For Weber, charisma is defined as, "[a] certain quality of an individual personality, by virtue of which he is set apart from ordinary men and treated as endowed with supernatural, superhuman, or at least specifically exceptional powers or qualities" (Weber, 1947, p.329). Freud explains these phenomena as the projection of the ego ideal onto the charismatic personality. Weber, influenced by Le Bon, notes also the fragility of the charismatic authority, which only remains in power by the constant demonstration of the strength and the successes of the leader. The mythological themes, for example the treason of the latter, sometimes do nothing but increase the fascination that it wields. The parallel with hypnosis, as Freud suggests it, is striking. In the novel by G. Steiner, The Portage to San Cristobal of A.H., the author arranges the warning to members of the Israeli commando charged with returning through the equatorial forest with a prisoner, who is none other than Hitler, around these lines: "You must not let him speak. [...] If he is able to speak, he will fool you and escape. [...] Do not look in his eyes. They say that they have a strange brilliance" (Steiner, 1981, pp. 33-34).

Whatever the case be in these variations, these phenomena, this "strange brilliance" evokes the etymology of charisma: the Greek word *charis* means "that which shines" and delights the eye physically—the external charm of a person, a face, a look.

It is always the thrill of the grandeur of the cause; its unique, messianic character, the obligation to total devotion of the faithful and the perfidy of the traitors and the adversaries that constitute the frame. One cannot but be struck by the resemblance of the language to another world, another time. The purity of the believers is opposed everywhere by the impurity of the adversary, health by malady, the God-Ideal by the machinations of Satan. The traitors, gunned down, struck down, are equal to rabid dogs in the language of Tehran as in the accounts of the Moscow trials or in the indictment of Rajk in Budapest, just as the executioner is universally the avenger-angel, brandishing the sword of Gabriel, lighting the purifying flame or striking the People with a fist. A few brushstrokes alters the images slightly through the ages, but they always suggest the vindictive omnipotence of the Righteous, stolen from the gods.

Action accompanies speech. The fanatic discourse is a communication made up of verbal language, as well as posture, mimics and movements: trembling, straightening up of the body, sometimes even convulsions accompanied by cries and shouts. A more detailed study could one day present the strange mimetic methods of fanaticism, its gesticulation even taken occasionally from mental illness or the ritual dances of men in trances and shamans.

If all of this is a caricature and if Freud makes us penetrate these shadowy regions of the subterranean life of men, as well as of man in our civilization, what could be the positive gains of such a penetration? To understand history better, to resist better the temptations of every kind of totalitarianism, the antechambers of fanaticism—to understand more deeply the subjects that move about these corridors or that which would slough off their fanatic aspect—to be sure; but also, last but not least, to recognize the fanatic temptations in each one of us. The more a science is shrouded by uncertainties, the less constraining the evidence, the more one is in the domain of the hypothesis than in the thesis or, particularly, the truths, the more the science—psychoanalysis, as that is what we are talking about—is an attempt at a cultural elaboration through profound interpersonal experiences in a specific situation which Freud called the psychoanalytic "cure"—then the stronger the desire, the temptation, to find something more sure, more practical, more clearly tangible, becomes. Thus, we easily find ourselves in the situation of having to defend this truth against the winds and the tides and being persecuted by all those who do not wish to enter directly into our way of reasoning, of seeing the world divvied up into good, right, reasonable, brothers and sisters, on one side, and evil on the other, those who demand more proof, who are skeptical, who try alternative discourses, who attack us, who question us. Our group is so strong—our ego ideal, as according to Freud, so reassuring—that whosoever infringes on this image becomes an enemy and those who, on the inside, propose any modification to the "religion" become, in the language of totalitarianism, revisionists, people to expel, motivated by the unconscious desire to keep the group pure and homogeneous and worthy of the projected ego ideal, and to distinguish it from all of the projected "evil". I mean that this is a temptation, but it is not far from having been realized in the course of history, in a more or less explicit manner. Psychoanalysts' strength could be to accept and contain the uncertainties, holding the tensions by accepting inevitable ambiguities in life.

SEEDS OF FANATICISM IN PSYCHOANALYSIS

It is possible to ask: Are there not, in the conception of the "psychoanalytic movement," the seeds of such a fanatic evolution? At the end of the first decade of the 1900s and the beginning of the next, Freud found himself the victim of an exclusion from the university despite the title of professor which he had finally obtained—and was not, according to his science, sufficiently reassured by his affiliation with B'nai Brith, which was a cultural association and a Jewish organization, as he had hoped to avoid that psychoanalysis become a "Jewish national affair" [Freud to

Abraham, May 3,1908]). He sought two things: a scientific basis, or even an intellectual certainty of his grasp of the dynamism of the conscious and, especially, the unconscious, life of man, which he had thought to have found in sexology (1905d) and in the theory of drives (1915c), and another certainty which would allow the survival of the psychoanalytical organization, practice, and science, which he no longer found in the existing academic institutions and which he would form, without a doubt, in the image of the "-isms" that surrounded him in the political, artistic, and cultural life of his Viennese surroundings (such as Austro-Marxism, Zionism, nationalism, Nazism, on one side, positivism, empirio-criticism, and all of the other cultural "-isms" on the other). But was he considered a scientist in that period of triumphant, empirical so-called "natural sciences"? He, in the face of the problems he was preoccupied with, often issued some tentative hypothesis and, in various following steps, showed himself more and more convinced, without adding new proofs, saying that "We are in the right." Such a procedure would be typical of philosophers, but a "natural scientist," as Freud wanted to be regarded, would aim at finding a fact and not an inner conviction. As an illustration, take for example, the history of the concept of the "instinct of death," which followed exactly this development. In a first step, he presented it as a mere hypothesis, and a few years later he wrote that he was fully convinced of it.

He didn't, however, want to be considered a philosopher either; nevertheless he founded the psychoanalytic movement. At the same time, he seemed a bit bothered, when Jones and Ferenczi proposed to create a secret Committee (Jones to Freud, July 30, 1912): didn't he say that it was a bit "infantile" ("knabenhaftes "), (Freud to Jones, August 1, 1912)? Doesn't this embarrassment express a kind of premonitory sentiment of something *unheimlich*, a sort of disturbing strangeness? He left behind the known forms of scientific organization, and even wondered if it would not be beneficial to join his psychoanalytic movement with the one of a Swiss apothecary, Alfred Knapp, called "International Order for Ethics and Culture." It was an enlightened and humanistic movement, comparable to that of the Freemasons, that propagated a-religious, humanistic, ethical, and cultural values. Encouraged by Ferenczi and

Jones, Freud abandoned this idea and opted, instead, to form an independent organization, keeping the values that he had previously envisioned. It is thus that the International Psychoanalytic Association (IPA) was born on the one hand, the Secret Committee on the other. In fact, the latter, formed in 1912, was also meant to be controlled by the president of the IPA at the time, C.G. Jung, who ended his term and severed ties with Freud in the same year (Freud and Jung, 1974).

The history of these two institutions has been written about many times from critical points of view (Grosskurth, 1991; Leitner, 1998). Further reflection reveals this movement, with its religious resonance of orthodoxy and heterodoxy, using methods of exclusion, and reminds us of the synagogue against Spinoza or the anathemas of church in the Middle Ages. The confessions and reconversions around the famous dramatic circular letter of Otto Rank's repentance (December 20, 1924, Lieberman, 1985, pp. 294-296), in which he expressed his wish to present the explanation of his conduct to the members of the Secret Committee "to apologize and make amends". He wrote: "From analytic interviews with Professor [Freud] (…) Professor found my explanations satisfactory and forgave me personally" (ibid., p. 249). But only a few days later, he retracted his words leaving even today's reader to feel how difficult it was for him to assert this position against his ego ideal of self-respect and independence on the one side and his idealization invested in Freud on the other. All of these phenomena were at the very borders of a scientific movement and touch the margins of the temptation to become a homogeneous fanatic group in possession of a sole, exclusive Truth. The question is not whether Freud was right to protect his development in a difficult and uncertain field, the exploration of the unconscious—by self-analysis and by other interpretive methods which he, himself, sometimes qualified as "speculations" (Freud, 1900a, p. 483; 1918a, pp. 77; 1920g, pp. 29; 1924d, p. 121; 1930a, p. 50). Our methods—for the majority of us—are not, however, immune to the regression of inheriting certainties while violently severing the Gordian knot. Thus we associate ourselves with a movement at the threshold of fanaticism, outside of intellectual discourse, while isolating us from the world in which we live, severing our contacts and seeking security within this isolation in the name of fidelity to the Freudian tradition. Could it be that our tradition is so close to the fanatic position, or else, is it rather a search for pluralism and dialogue with contemporary sciences—as Freud had always fostered contacts with neurological sciences, linguistics, sexology, endocrinology, anthropology, and, with artists like poets, novelists, and writers –? A reflection on fanaticism is not only a reflection on our patients, disgusted by every kind of sectarianism and bearing the wounds of depression, even sometimes nostalgia, after breaking with these "religions", but also on ourselves with our own nostalgia for intellectual and affective security, which we cannot (because of our ideals!) allow ourselves to cultivate in a fanatic posture.

We must see ourselves as potential fanatics. Our scientific perspective is not universally accepted: our scientific credibility and our references are challenged. There are those fanatics who interrogate us in a fanatic manner: "Freud bashing" has much to say on this topic. There could be economic reasons behind every such attack, for example competition for economic resources and possibly envy and jealousy, or other personal reasons. But this is not the whole story. There are promises about which we have boasted but have not kept, an uncertainty overcompensated by claims without sufficient proof, as well as some confusion between hypotheses and scientific facts: All of these excesses are sustained by our underlying emotions.

In our "illusion of group" (Freud, 1921c, p. 94), the ideal image of the leader is so reassuring that it becomes an important positive connection. Ernst Falzeder (2015) had the excellent idea of demonstrating how psychoanalytic groups and "schools" are established around a charismatic and reassuring personality with which the members of the group conduct their didactic analyses, thus forming "genealogical trees". In this manner, the whole group has been profoundly affected and influenced by the analyst. It is enough to analyze the bibliographies of psychoanalytic articles to discover that the majority of references are made up of the group to which the author belongs. For polemical reasons, a few other thinkers are cited, but they are apparently known more by hearsay than by careful study or experiment.

Inter-group communication and personal stimulation within these groups is facilitated, which is certainly a positive aspect. However, it is also undeniable that the narcissistic confirmation of being one of the "initiated" and the object of a mutual admiration, the member of the foremost group regarding psychoanalytic knowledge (the most scientific, for example), is a highly stabilizing factor. One can easily infer the organizational and political consequences from this (King and Steiner, 1991), and the atmosphere created can come very close to the scope of fanaticism. Fortunately, this boundary is rarely transgressed, and the paranoid projections and concerns are kept under effective control. Even still, the "group illusion" vested in the specific branch generates a considerable loss of information, exchange, and ultimate impoverishment.

In struggling to understand human nature, Freud taught us to first examine ourselves. Wasn't the most important teaching of Freud *Gnothi Heauton*—Know Thyself (Delphic maxim, Temple of Apollo, Delphi)?

FANATICISM STILL ALIVE

Fanaticism is alive and well today. Fanaticism shows itself at the root of hateful attitudes towards others, foremost in political and ideological convictions of larger populations. This, I discovered also in everyday life even in my "civilized" environment. As a teenager it became more and more striking to me and it was a surprise to become sensitive to the extraordinary and brutal evolutions in Europe, which made the twentieth century hell for a majority of people entangled in wars and persecutions. Moreover, even in our so-called "evolved" society, fanatical mentality leaves its trace everywhere. Finally, on a larger scale and in the twenty-first century, we find ourselves confronted with dramatic political and military situations. We are witness to the culmination of fervent nationalistic and religious forces of new levels of extremes, recalling the two great World Wars or, if possible, even worse, having access to and deploying a level of violence possibly never before seen. Thus, as in "repetition compulsion," we see the destructive forces of the unconscious reappear everywhere in a manner that becomes extremely unsettling.

Only a hard work of understanding all these underground forces potentially acting in each of us may allow the situation to improve, even against those other economic, political and societal factors that are making our endeavors to change difficult, but not impossible.

Epilogue

Life isn't about finding yourself;
it is about creating yourself.
GEORGE BERNARD SHAW

Habent sua fata libelli—books make their own destiny; just as with this book. It began as notes for my family, my wife and my children—with some anecdotes from them included as well. I kept hearing people around me say, "You should also mention this or that in your notation", and spontaneous thoughts inserted themselves into my own observations. While rereading them attentively, the possibility dawned on me of scribbling down my *Einfälle* (which could be best translated as "incidents"),[52] and the experience of a more generalized reflection was born out of them. In Central Europe, writing diaries was commonplace; this is probably how many writers attempted to escape the otherwise omnipresent censorship. Perhaps irrationally, and without thinking about it explicitly, I also do tend to avoid the criticism and censorship of my colleagues who could judge whether I am in accordance with them, or at least with a majority of people "who know…"

I thought about the autobiographical writers we find among psychoanalysts. I pen in a different style from Ferenczi in his *Diary* (1985) and

---

[52] From the Latin from the verb incidere, from in- 'upon' + cadere 'to fall': falling upon.

Bion in his *A Memoir of the Future* (1990), but I am still struck by the fact that although Ferenczi underwent analysis with Freud, "the best" possible in his time, and Bion underwent analysis with Melanie Klein—also an impressive personality—, nevertheless they wanted, and even perhaps needed, to write about themselves! I also write after three psychoanalyses, why? Both, Ferenczi and Bion were, I realized, traumatized persons. Like me. Writing all this allowed me to meditate about my own traumatism, thus my little-ego, [Ich-lein] is now satisfied, delighted.

My hope is that it also might be interesting to read about the life of a psychoanalyst with an unusual background. Unusual, I was always: you could see it in the precedent narrative of my self-reflections. A maverick living his own life, not the one of others; not one to follow authoritarian ego-alien prescriptions. In a sense, non-conformist, unconventional, sometimes rebellious; one who decided to live the life of his own dreams.

Could this conception of life be of interest to other people? Could it encourage them to be themselves? Good or bad fortune is of our own making, so let's make it good. But, how can we make it good? First by understanding oneself better, I'd say.

To understand human beings so that I might be better able to help them understand themselves: this was my hope, which led me to my studies in psychology, philosophy, and finally, medicine. Even today, it seems to me that it is the renewal of ideas—that is, scientific progress—that leads us to a better and better understanding of man, and potential developments for therapeutic practice. A broad anthropology helped me, as well. It encompasses the biological bases linked to brain function, ethology (comparative study of animals), genetics, the impetus given by Darwin, Freud and 20th century thinkers, cultural and social psychologies. Moreover philosophy and literature both record and share these gains in the cultural evolution of different human societies. From Plato and the various ancient schools of philosophy, to our more recent philosophers like Schopenhauer and Nietzsche, Popper and Wittgenstein, not forgetting the ideas offered by the world's religions (from meditation to mindfulness; William James[53], etc.),

---

[53] Philosopher, physician and the first educator to offer a psychology course in the United States.

all these paths offer us the significant prospect of exploring the inner world, especially its emotional and relational background, often through their irrational manifestations.

In fact, this work has not much to do with medicine at all, even though historical developments tend to link psychoanalysis with medicine. A part of these considerations developed inside medicine, addressed to apparent "symptoms" like depressive moods, digestive disturbances, sleeplessness and in similar "applications" to health problems and others remain in the domains of other methods in order to improve satisfaction in life.

What, then, were my instruments for this exploration in listening to others and to myself? Hearing and understanding these discourses require us to rely on precise semiology and semantics. In this context, metaphor becomes a central concept in order to grasp the connotation of the terms used in these narratives, i.e. the associative field surrounding the terms expressed in the "free associations". What is called meta-phor, when speaking about writings, is designated in a relationship as trans-fer (Freud's Über-tragung). *Übertragung* has strictly the same meaning as meta-phor. In *Über-tragung*, the subject addresses himself to me not as I am, but as an internal image, for example, that of his father, projected on me. In both cases, *Übertragung* and metaphor, there is the same use of resemblance (or, at least partial resemblance). There is the un-logical, the irrational, that we discover as co-determinant in what is uttered, of which the unconscious is the part that we can only seldom directly recognize. But we may discover, little by little, that these associations lead us to the elements of our past that determined—then—our thinking, our decisions, and through which many important events (our choices) made us who we became throughout our past and who we are now, as a result. This transformative work gives us a more coherent sense of ourselves.

Coming to the end of this writing, I realize to which point I became fascinated with trying to understand myself and to help my fellow humans to do the same. This introspection allows me to touch the important aspects of what corrodes well-being in our world: disenchantment and discontent transmitted from generation to generation without their being aware of it, not having the metaphors to express and understand it. All this is tied to changes imposed or proven necessary which generate constraining anxiety toward adapting to new situations in life, in general. Shifts in life circumstances, losses, particularly those related to family, which result in burdensome solitude, even as early as infancy; the pressures of maturity, the sufferings tied to heightened competition, the hunger for power, and firm fanatic beliefs; and then, a thousand other causes of worry accompany us even in advanced age, in old age. To describe them all would require another book (the sequel to this one?). I am convinced, from my experience, that in most cases, understanding oneself allows us to succeed in creating satisfaction and that self-reflection is a realistic, promising path toward inner harmony, and fulfillment. I have come to the point now, in my attempt to understand myself, to ask you, dear reader, to participate in this endeavor as well, in order to reach through understanding (analysis), for myself and for you as well, peace and compassion.

Bibliographical References[54]

Anzieu, Didier (1986): *Freud's Self-Analysis*. London, Hogarth Press.

Bion, Wilfred R. (1962): *Learning from experience*. London, Karnac, 1984.

Bolterauer, Lambert (1975): Der Fanatismus. *Psyche, 29*: 287-315.

Brabant, Eva, Falzeder, Ernst, Giampieri-Deutsch, Patrizia (Eds.) (1993): *The Correspondence of Sigmund Freud and Sándor Ferenczi*. Volume 1, 1908-1914. Scientific supervision André Haynal. Cambridge, MA/London, Harvard Univ. Press.

Camus, Albert (2005): *Myth of Sisyphus*. New York, Penguin books (1942).

Chasseguet-Smirgel, Janine (1975): *The Ego Ideal: A Psychoanalytic Essay on the Malady of the Ideal*. New York, W W Norton & Co Inc., 1985.

Chertok, Léon, de Saussure, Raymond (1973): *Naissance du psychanalyste. De Mesmer à Freud* [Birth of the Psychoanalyst: From Mesmer to Freud]. Paris, Payot.

Donnet, Jean-Luc, Green, André (1973): *L'enfant de ça*. Paris, Minuit.

---

[54] S. E. refers to The Standard Edition of the Complete Psychological Works of Sigmund Freud, James Strachey (Ed.). London, Hogarth Press, 1953-1974.

Eliot, Thomas Stearns (1941): *"Four Quartets"*. Reed. Boston, MA, Mariner Books/Harcourt, 1968.

Falzeder, Ernst, Brabant, Eva (Eds.) (1996): *The Correspondence of Sigmund Freud and Sándor Ferenczi.* Volume 2, 1914-1919. Scientific supervision André Haynal. Cambridge, MA/London, Harvard Univ. Press.

Falzeder, Ernst, Brabant, Eva (Eds.) (2000): *The Correspondence of Sigmund Freud and Sándor Ferenczi.* Volume 3, 1920-1933. Scientific supervision André Haynal. Cambridge, MA/London, Harvard Univ. Press.

Falzeder, Ernst, (Ed.) (2002): *The Complete Correspondence of Sigmund Freud and Karl Abraham (1907-1925).* London, Karnac.

Falzeder, Ernst (2015): *Psychoanalytic Filiations: Mapping the Psychoanalytic Movement.* London, Karnac.

Fejtö, François (1997): *Hongrois et juifs. Une histoire millénaire d'un couple singulier (1000-1997).* Paris, Balland.

Ferenczi, Sándor (1916): *First Contributions to Psycho-analysis.* London, Hogarth, 1952 reprint.

Ferenczi, Sándor (1926): *Further Contributions to the Theory and Technique of Psycho-analysis.* London, Hogarth, 1950 reprint.

Ferenczi, Sándor (1955): *Final Contributions to the Problems and Methods of Psycho-analysis.* London, Hogarth, 1994 reprint.

Freud, Sigmund (1900a): The Interpretation of Dreams. S. E. 4-5, 1953.

Freud, Sigmund (1905d): Three Essays. S. E. 7: 135-243, 1953.

Freud, Sigmund (1915c): Instincts and their Vicissitudes. S. E. 14: 117-140, 1957.

Freud, Sigmund (1917e): Mourning and Melancholia. S. E. 14: 243-258, 1957.

Freud, Sigmund (1918a): The Taboo of Virginity. S. E. 11: 193-208, 1957.

Freud, Sigmund (1920g): Beyond the Pleasure Principle. S. E. 18: 7-64, 1955.

Freud, Sigmund (1921c): Group Psychology and the Analysis of the Ego. S. E. 18: 69-143, 1955.

Freud, Sigmund (1924d): The Dissolution of the Oedipus Complex. *S. E.* 19: 173-179, 1961.

Freud, Sigmund (1927c): The Future of an Illusion. *S. E. 21*: 5-56, 1961.

Freud, Sigmund (1930a [1929]): Civilization and its Discontents. *S. E. 21*: 64-145, 1961.

Freud, Sigmund (1933b [1932]): Why War? *S. E. 22*: 203-215, 1964.

Freud, Sigmund (1939a): Moses and Monotheism: Three Essays. *S. E. 23*: 7-137, 1964.

Freud, Sigmund, Jung, Carl G. (1974): *The Freud / Jung Letters: The Correspondence between Sigmund Freud and C.G. Jung.* Princeton, Princeton University Press.

Granoff, Wladimir (2001): *Lacan, Ferenczi et Freud.* Paris, Gallimard.

Green, Andre (1995): Has Sexuality Anything To Do With Psychoanalysis?. *Int. J. Psycho-Anal.,* 76:871-883.

Grosskurth, Phyllis (1991): *The Secret Ring: Freud's Inner Circle and the Politics of Psychoanalysis.* Boston, Addison-Wesley Pub.

Grubrich-Simitis, Ilse (Ed.) (1987): *A Phylogenetic Fantasy: Overview of the Transference Neuroses. A newly discovered manuscript Sigmund Freud [1915].* Cambridge, MA, Belknap Press/Harvard University Press.

Haldane, John Burdon Sanderson (1932): *The Inequality of Man and Other Essays.* Philadelphia, R. West/London, Chatto & Windus.

Haynal, André (1985): *Depression and creativity.* New York, International Universities Press.

Haynal, André (1988): *The technique at issue. Controversies in psychoanalysis from Freud and Ferenczi to Michael Balint.* GB edition London, Karnac, 1988, U.S. edition New York, New York University Press, 1989.

Haynal, André (1989): *Controversies in Psychoanalytic Method. From Freud and Ferenczi to Michael Balint.* New York, New York University Press.

Haynal, André (1993): Ferenczi and the origins of psychoanalytic technique, *in*: Lewis Aron, Adrienne Harris (Eds): *The legacy of Sándor Ferenczi.* Hillsdale, N.J., The Analytic Press, pp. 53-74.

Haynal, André (1993): Introduction, *in*: Brabant, Eva, Falzeder, Ernst, Giampieri-Deutsch, Patrizia (Eds.), 1993, v. supra.

Haynal, André (2002): *Disappearing and Reviving. Sándor Ferenczi in the History of Psychoanalysis.* London, Karnac.

Haynal, André, Mészáros, Judit (2012): *Nemek és igenek. Magántörténelem és pszichoanalízis.* Budapest, Oriold és Tsai.

Haynal, André, Pasini, Willy (1978): *Abrégé de médecine psychosomatique.* Paris, Masson.

King, Pearl, Steiner, Riccardo (Eds) (1991): *The Freud-Klein Controversies 1941-45.* London, Routledge.

Koestler, Arthur (1978): *Janus. A Summing Up.* New York, Random House, 1979.

Lacan, Jacques (1956): The Situation of Psychoanalysis and the Training of the Psychoanalyst, *in*: Ecrits. New York, W. W. Norton & Company, 2007.

Laplanche, Jean, Pontalis, Jean-Bernard (1967): *Vocabulaire de la psychanalyse.* Paris, Presses universitaires de France.

Le Bon, Gustave (1895): *The Crowd: A Study of the Popular Mind.* New York, Dover Publications, 2002.

Leitner, Marina (1998): *Der Konflikt zwischen Sigmund Freud und Otto Rank. Ein Schlüsselkonflikt für die Entwicklung der Psychotherapie des 20.Jahrhunderts.* Vienna, Turia & Kant.

Lieberman, E. James (1985): *Acts of Will.* New York, Free Press.

Lloyd Mayer, Elisabeth (2007): *Extraordinary Knowing.* New York, Bantam Books.

Merton M. Gill (Ed.) (1967): *The collected papers of David Rapaport.* New York, Basis Books.

Paskauskas, Andrew R. (Ed.) (1993): *The Complete Correspondence of Sigmund Freud and Ernest Jones 1908-1939*. Cambridge, MA/London, Harvard Univ. Press.

Pontalis, Jean-Bertrand (1968): *Après Freud*. Paris, Gallimard.

Rangell, Leo (1974): Psychoanalytic perspectives leading currently to the syndrome of the compromise of integrity. *Int. J. Psycho-Anal.*, 55/1: 3-12.

Reich, Wilhelm. (1933): *The Mass Psychology of Fascism*. New York, Farrar, Straus & Giroux, 1970.

Steiner, George (1981): *The Portage to San Cristobal of A.H.* London/Boston, Faber & Faber.

Szegő, Júlia (1965): *Embernek maradni. Bartók Béla életregénye* [Keeping our Humanity: The Life Story of Béla Bartók]. Budapest, Zenemű kiadó.

Swift, Jonathan (1726): *Gulliver's Travels*. New York, Dover Publications, 1996.

Vermorel, Henri, Vermorel, Madeleine (1993): *Sigmund Freud et Romain Rolland, correspondance 1923-1936*. Paris, P.U.F.

Weber, Maximillan (1947): *The Theory of Social Economic Organization*. Chapter: "The Nature of Charismatic Authority and its Routinization". London, Oxford University Press.

Wenninger, Florian, Dreidemy, Lucile (2013): *Das Dollfuß/Schuschnigg-Regime 1933-1938*. Wien, Böhlau.

www.ingramcontent.com/pod-product-compliance
Lightning Source LLC
Chambersburg PA
CBHW070615300426
44113CB00010B/1539